A CAMINO PILGRIM'S GUIDE

Sarria - Santiago - Finisterre

Including **Muxía camino circuit**

*A Practical & Mystical Manual
for the Modern Day Pilgrim*

maps • mapas • karten
mappe • cartes • kaarten • mapy

John Brierley

© John Brierley 2016

First edition published in 2016. Includes revised elements from A Pilgrim's Guide to
the Camino Finisterre (first published in 2001).

ISBN 978-1-84409-682-4

British Library Cataloguing-in-Publication Data.
A catalogue record for this book is available from the British Library.

Printed and bound in the European Union

Published by
CAMINO GUIDES
An imprint of Findhorn Press Ltd
117-121 High Street,
Forres IV36 1AB
Scotland
Tel: +44(0)1309 690 582
Fax: +44(0)131 777 2711

Email: info@findhornpress.com
www.findhornpress.com
www.caminoguides.com

Map Legend: Symbols used in this guide:

Total km — Total distance for stage map
— Adjusted for climb (100m vertical = additional 0.5km)
(850m) **Alto ▲** — Contours / High point of each stage
< A H > — Intermediate accommodation (*often less busy / quieter*)
◄ 3.5 — Precise distance between points (3.5 km = ± 1 hour)
→●150m > / ^ / < — Interim distances •150m turn right> / s/o straight on^ / <left

........../.......... — Path or track (*green*: natural path / *grey:* concrete or *senda*)
—○— — Secondary road (*grey*: asphalt) / Roundabout *rotonda*
━━**N-11**━━ — Main road [N-] *Nacional* (*red*: additional traffic and hazard)
══**A-1**══ — Motorway *autopista* (*blue*: conventional motorway colour)
++++++++● — Railway *ferrocarril* / Station *estación*

● ● ● ● ● — Main route (*yellow*: ± 80% of pilgrims)
● ● ● ● ● — Scenic route (*green*: more remote / less pilgrims)
● ● ● ● ● — Optional detour *desvío* (*turquoise*) to point of interest
● ● ● ● ● — Alternative road route (*grey*: more asphalt)
X ? ❗ — Crossing *cruce* / Option *opción* / Extra care *¡cuidado!*

↑ ⋇ ♦ — Windmill / Viewpoint *punto de vista* / Radio mast
▪—▪/▪—▪ — National boundary / Provincial boundary *límite provincial*
〜/〜 — River *río* / Stream *arroyo*
◯/◯ — Sea or lake *Mar o lago* / Woodland *bosques*
♦ ♦ † — Church *iglesia* / Chapel *capilla* / Wayside cross *cruceiro*

🜂 ☕ 🏪 — Drinking font *fuente agua potable* / Café / Shop *minimercado*
menú *V.* — *menú peregrino* 3 course meal + wine / *V. Vegetariano*
🛈 🏛 ✕ — Tourist office *turismo* / Manor house *casa señorial* / Picnic
✚ ✚ ✉ — Pharmacy *farmacia* / Hospital / Post office *correos*
✈ 🚏 ⛽ — Airport / Bus station *estación de autobús* / *gasolinera*
♠ XIIᵗʰc — Ancient monument / 12th century

A❶ **J** — Pilgrim hostel(s) *Albergue* / Youth hostel *Juventude*
H P C — Hotels *H-H*""""€30-90 / Pension *P*"€20+ / B&B *CR* €35+
⟨H⟩ ⟨A⟩ ⟨J⟩ — (off route accommodation *alojamiento fuera de ruta*)
[32] — Number of bed spaces (usually bunk beds *literas*)
[÷4]+ — ÷ number of rooms / + additional private rooms €20+
Par. — Parish hostel *Parroquial* donation / €5
Conv. — Convent or monastery hostel *donativo* / €5
Muni. — Municipal hostel €5+
Xunta — Galician government *Xunta* hostel €6
Asoc. — Association hostel €7+
Priv. (*) — Private hostel (network*) €10-15
Prices (low season) average; for comparison purposes only
⬜ — Town plan *plan de la ciudad* with page number
(Pop.–Alt. m) — Town population and altitude in metres
— City suburbs *suburbios de la ciudad* (*grey*)
— Historical centre *centro histórico* (*brown*)

Introduction: There is too much paraphernalia in our lives – in an effort to lighten the load we have produced this slim hybrid edition with multilingual maps. This has been made possible by the selfless work of pilgrim associations that have way-marked the route such that, today, we need only the barest information to get us to our destination. It would be difficult to get lost if we remain present to each moment and attentive for the yellow arrows that point the way to Santiago and Finisterre – mindfulness is the key. Take time to familiarise yourself with the map symbols opposite.

The standard and cost of pilgrim accommodation ranges from Xunta hostels offering basic facilities from €6 (no prior booking) to private hostels from €10+ but often with additional facilities such as washing *lavadoras* and drying machines *secadora* - the latter a real boon in wet weather. The cost of hotels also varies widely depending on season; many offer a pilgrim discount but ask *before* booking. A basic 3 course meal with wine *menú peregrino* costs around €9.

The multilingual maps recognise the international fellowship of the camino. This helps to foster a sense of camaraderie and communion; a shared spiritual intention that lies at the heart of pilgrimage. It is this transcendent focus that distinguishes pilgrimage from long distance walking. If you require detailed notes on preparation, source an appropriate guidebook such as the companion book *A Pilgrim's Guide to the Camino Francés*.

All of us travel two paths simultaneously; the outer path along which we haul our body and the inner pathway of soul. We need to be mindful of both and take time to prepare ourselves accordingly. The traditional way of the pilgrim is to travel alone, by foot, carrying all the material possessions we might need for the journey ahead. This provides the first lesson for the pilgrim – to leave behind all that is superfluous and to travel with only the barest necessities. Preparation for the inner path is similar – we start by letting go of psychic waste accumulated over the years such as resentments, prejudices and outmoded belief systems. Walking with an open mind and open heart allows us to assimilate the lessons to be found along this ancient Path of Enquiry.

We have been asleep a long time. Despite the chaotic world around us, or perhaps because of it, something is stirring us to awaken from our collective amnesia. A sign of this awakening is the number of people drawn to walk the caminos. The hectic pace of modern life, experienced not only in our work but also our family and social lives, spins us ever outwards away from our centre. We have allowed ourselves to be thrown onto the surface of our lives – mistaking busy-ness for aliveness, but this superficial existence is inherently unsatisfying.

Pilgrimage offers us an opportunity to slow down and allow some spaciousness into our lives. In this quieter space we can reflect on the deeper significance of our lives and the reasons why we came here. The camino encourages us to ask the perennial question – Who am I? And, crucially, it provides time for answers to be understood and integrated. So don't rush the camino – take the time it takes because it may well prove a pivotal turning point in your life.

Whichever route we take, our ultimate Destination is assured. The only choice we have is how long it takes us to arrive *buen camino*.

John Brierley

Claves para las leyendas del mapa:

Total km — Distancia total de la etapa indicada

— Adaptado para el desnivel (100 m verticales = a 0,5 km adicionales)

(850m) **Alto ▲** — Curva de desnivel / Punto más elevado de cada etapa

< Ⓐ Ⓗ > — Alojamiento intermedio (*menos ocupado / más tranquilo*)

◄ 3.5 — Distancia exacta entre puntos (3,5 km = ± 1 hora de camino)

—●150m > / ^ / < — Distancias parciales: a150 m a la derecha> / seguir recto / <a la izquierda

·········· / ·········· — Camino o sendero (*verde*: caminos naturales / *gris*: hormigón)

—○— — Carretera secundaria (*gris*: asfalto) / Rotonda

N-11 — Carretera principal [N-] (*rojo*: mayor tráfico y peligro)

A-1 — Autopista (*azul*: color habitual)

+++++++●— Vía de tren / / Estación de ferrocarril

● ● ● ● ● — Ruta principal (*amarillo*: ± 80% peregrinos)

● ● ● ● ● — Ruta escénica (*verde*: más alejada / menos peregrinos)

● ● ● ● ● — Ruta por carretera (*gris*: más asfalto)

● ● ● ● ● — Rodeo opcional a un punto de interés (*turquesa*)

X ? ❶ — Cruce / Punto de Opción / Atención especial

✝ ☀ ♀ — Molino de viento / Punto de vista / Antena de radio

·—·/·—· — Frontera estatal / Límites de provinciales

~ / ~ — Río / Arroyo

◯ / ◯ — Lago o estuario / Bosque

✝ ✝ ✝ — Iglesia / Capilla / Crucero

Ⓕ ☕ ♨ — Fuente de agua potable / Café / Mini-mercado

menú *V.* — Menu peregrino ±€9 / *V.* Vegetariano

Ⓘ ⌂ ✕ — Turismo / Casa señorial / Picnic

✚ ✚ ✉ — Farmacia / Hospital / Oficina de correos

✈ 🚌 ⛽ — Aeropuerto / Estación de autobús / Gasolinera

●● XII[th]c — Monumento histórico / Siglo XII

Ⓐ❶ Ⓙ — Albergue(s) de peregrinos / Albergue juvenil

Ⓗ Ⓟ Ⓒ — Hoteles *H–H***** €30–90 / Pensión *P* €20+ / *Casa rural CR* €35+

Ⓗ Ⓐ Ⓙ — Alojamiento *fuera* de ruta

[32] — Número de plazas de cama (normalmente literas)

[÷4]+ — ÷ número de dormitorios + *también habitaciones privadas €20+*

Par. — Albergue parroquial *donación* / €5

Conv. — Albergue en un convento o monasterio *donación* / €5+

Muni. — Albergue municipal €5+

Xunta — Albergue de la Xunta de Galicia €6

Asoc. — Albergue de una asociación €7+

Priv. (*) — Albergue privado (de la Red de Albergues*) €10 (incl.=+desayuno)

Todos los precios son aproximados y sólo a efectos comparativos

▭ — Plano de ciudad

(Pop.–Alt. m) — Población – Altitud en metros

▬ — Periferia (*gris*)

▬ — Centro Histórico (*marrón*)

Introducción: En las vidas de todos nosotros hay un exceso de parafernalia. Con la pretensión de aligerar la carga, hemos creado esta delgada edición con mapas multilingües. Ello ha sido posible gracias al trabajo desinteresado de las asociaciones de peregrinos que han señalizado el recorrido de tal forma que, hoy en día, tan solo necesitamos la información más básica para alcanzar nuestro destino. Resulta difícil perderse si en todo momento permanecemos concentrados y atentos a las flechas amarillas que apuntan en dirección a Santiago y Finisterre: en la concentración está la clave. Tómate un tiempo para familiarizarte con los símbolos del mapa que hallarás en la página de enfrente.

El estándar y el costo de alojamiento peregrino varía de los albergues de la Xunta que ofrece servicios básicos de € 6 (sin reserva previa) a los albergues privados a partir de € 10 + pero a menudo con servicios adicionales tales como lavadoras y secadoras. Un menú peregrino comprende una comida básica de 3 platos con vino a un costo de alrededor de 9 €.

Estos mapas multilingües son un reconocimiento al compañerismo internacional del camino. Éste favorece el sentimiento de camaradería y comunión; una intención espiritual compartida que yace en el corazón de la peregrinación. Es esta focalización transcendente lo que distingue al peregrinaje del senderismo de larga distancia.

Todos recorremos dos caminos simultáneamente: el camino exterior, por el que arrastramos nuestro cuerpo, y el camino interior del alma. Debemos ser conscientes de los dos y tomarnos el tiempo para prepararnos adecuadamente. El camino tradicional del peregrino es viajar solo, a pie, cargando con todas las posesiones materiales que podamos necesitar en el viaje que tenemos por delante. Esto brinda la primera lección al peregrino: dejar atrás todo lo superfluo y viajar tan sólo con lo estrictamente necesario. La preparación para el camino interior es similar: comenzamos soltando la basura psíquica acumulada a lo largo de los años, como resentimientos, prejuicios y sistemas de creencias pasados de moda. Con una mente y un corazón abiertos asimilaremos con mayor facilidad las lecciones con las que nos encontraremos a lo largo de este Camino de las Averiguaciones.

Llevamos mucho tiempo dormidos. Pese al caótico mundo que nos rodea, o tal vez a causa de él, hay algo que nos sacude para que despertemos de nuestra amnesia colectiva. Una señal de este despertar es el número de personas que se sienten atraídas por hacer los caminos. El ritmo frenético de la vida moderna, que experimentamos no sólo en el trabajo sino también en nuestra vida familiar y en la social, hace que cada vez revoloteamos más lejos de nuestro centro. Hemos consentido en ser arrojados a la superficie de nuestras vidas, al confundir estar ocupados con estar vivos, pero esta existencia superficial resulta intrínsecamente insatisfactoria.

La peregrinación nos brinda la oportunidad de reducir el ritmo y de dotar a nuestras vidas de una cierta amplitud. En este espacio más tranquilo se puede reflexionar acerca del significado más profundo de nuestras vidas y las razones por las que hemos venido aquí. El camino nos anima a hacernos la pregunta perenne: ¿quién soy? Y, lo que resulta crucial, nos proporciona el tiempo para poder comprender y asimilar las respuestas. Así que no te apresures en recorrer el camino: tómate el tiempo que sea necesario, porque podría resultar ser el punto de inflexión de tu vida.

Buen camino !

Zeichenerklärung:

Total km	Gesamtentfernung für angezeigte Etappe
▲	An Höhenunterschied angepasst (100 m Höhe = zusätzliche 0,5 km)
_(850m)_**Alto▲**	Etappenprofil / Höchster Punkt jeder Etappe
< Ⓐ Ⓗ >	Unterkunft unterwegs (*oft weniger beschäftigt / leiser*)
◀ **3.5**	Genaue Entfernung zwischen Punkten (3,5 km = ± 1 Stunde Wandern)
●150m > / ^ / <	Zwischenentfernungen – in 150 m nach rechts> / geradeaus^ /
	<nach links
⬝⬝⬝⬝⬝⬝ / ⬝⬝⬝⬝⬝⬝	Weg oder Pfad (*grün*: natürliche Wege / *grau*: beton)
═══○═══	Nebenstraße (*grau*: Asphalt) / Kreisverkehr
═══**N-11**═══	Hauptstraße [N-] (*rot*: mehr Verkehr und größere Gefahr)
═══**A-1**═══	Autobahn (*blau*: herkömmliche Farbe)
+++++++●	Bahn / Bahnhof
● ● ● ● ●	Hauptroute (*gelb*: ± 80% pilger / vorwiegend Wege)
● ● ● ● ●	Route mit Ausblick (*grün*: abgelegener / weniger Pilger)
● ● ● ● ●	Landstraßen-Route (*grau*: mehr Asphalt)
● ● ● ● ●	Möglicher Abstecher desvío zu Sehenswürdigkeit (*türkis*)
Ⓧ ❓ ❗	Kreuzung / Optionspunkt / Besondere Vorsicht
↑ ☀ ↑	Windrad / Aussichtspunkt / Antennenmast
▪—▪/▪—▪	Landesgrenze / Provinzgrenze
∼ / ∼	Fluss / Bach
⬭ / ⬭	See oder Flussmündung / Wald
✝ ⸶ ✝	Kirche / Kapelle / Kreuz am Wegesrand
⊙ ▬ ♨	Trinkwasser-Quelle / Café Bar / Mini-Markt
menú V.	Restaurant mit Pilgermenü *menú* / Vegetarisch
🅩 🏠 ✕	Tourismus / Herrenhaus / Picknick-Tisch
➊ ➋ ✉	Apotheke / Krankenhaus / Post
⊕ 🅗 🅟	Flughafen / Busbahnhof / Tankstelle
⁂ XII[th]c	Altes Denkmal / 12. Jahrhundert
🅐① Ⓙ	Pilgerherberge(n) / Jugendherberge
🄷 🄿 🄲	Hotel *H*-*H***** €30–90 /Pension *P* €20+ / Zimmer Incl.** *CR* €35+
Ⓗ Ⓐ Ⓙ	*Unterkunft abseits der Route*
[32]	Anzahl der Bettplätze (gewöhnlich Etagenbetten)
[÷4]+	÷ Anzahl der Schlafsäle + *auch Privatzimmer* €20+
Par.	Gemeinde-Herberge (Kirchengemeinde) Spende *donación (€5)*
Conv.	Klosterherberge Spende *donación (€5+)*
Muni.	Städtische Herberge €5+
Xunta	Herberge der Landesregierung Galiziens (Xunta) €6
Asoc.	Herberge einer Vereinigung €7+
Priv. (*)	Private Herberge (privates Netzwerk*) €10+ / Incl.** mit Frühstück
	Alle Preise sind annähernd und nur zum Vergleich angegeben
▭	Stadtplan
(Pop.–Alt. m)	Außenbezirke (*grau*)
	Altstadt centro histórico (*braun*)
▭	Stadtbevölkerung – Höhe in Metern

Einführung: Wir alle haben zu viel Trödel in unserem Leben – in dem Bemühen, das Gewicht zu reduzieren, haben wir diese schlanke edition mit mehrsprachigen Karten hergestellt. Ermöglicht wurde dies durch die selbstlose Arbeit von Pilgerorganisationen, die die Route dergestalt markiert haben, dass wir heute nur die grundlegendste Information brauchen, um an unser Ziel zu gelangen. Es ist schwer, sich zu verlaufen; wir müssen nur in jedem Moment gegenwärtig sein und auf die gelben Pfeile achten, die den Weg nach Santiago und Finisterre weisen – Achtsamkeit ist der Schlüssel. Nimm dir Zeit, dich mit den Karten-Symbolen auf der gegenüberliegenden Seite vertraut zu machen.

Der Standard und die Kosten der Pilger Unterkunft variiert von *Xunta* Hostels bieten grundlegende Einrichtungen ab € 6 (kein Vorreservierung) an private Hostels ab € 10 +, aber oft mit zusätzlichen Einrichtungen wie Waschmaschinen und Trockner. Eine grundlegende 3-Gänge-Menü mit Wein *menú peregrino* kostet ca. € 9.

Die mehrsprachigen Karten würdigen die internationale Gemeinschaft des Camino. Dieser för¬dert das Gefühl von Freundschaft und Vereinigung; ein ge¬meinsames geistiges Ansinnen, das im Herzen der Wallfahrt liegt. Es ist dieser Fokus auf das Transzendente, was eine Wallfahrt vom Fernwandern unter¬scheidet.

Wir alle reisen gleichzeitig auf zwei Wegen; der äußere, entlang dessen wir unseren Körper schleppen, und der innere Weg der Seele. Wir müssen uns beider bewusst sein und uns die Zeit nehmen für eine entsprechende Vorbereitung. Traditionsgemäß ist der Weg des Wallfahrers eine Reise zu Fuß, alleine; wir tragen allen materiellen Besitz, den wir für die bevorstehende Fahrt benötigen mögen, mit uns. Dies bringt auch die erste Lektion für den Pilger – alles Überflüssige hinter sich zu lassen und nur mit dem wahrhaft Notwendigen zu reisen. Die Vorbereitung für den inneren Weg ist ähnlich – sie beginnt mit dem Ablegen vom psychischen Müll, der sich über die Jahre angehäuft hat, wie Groll, Vorurteile und überholte Glaubenssysteme. Mit offenem Verstand und offenem Herzen werden wir umso leichter die Lehren aufnehmen, die entlang dieses uralten Weges der Suche gefunden werden können.

Wir haben lange geschlafen. Trotz der chaotischen Welt um uns herum, oder vielleicht gerade ihretwegen, schüttelt uns etwas, auf dass wir aus unserer kollektiven Amnesie erwachen. Ein Zeichen dieses Erwachens ist die Anzahl der Menschen, die sich angezogen fühlen, die Caminos zu erwandern. Das hektische Tempo des modernen Lebens, das wir nicht nur in unserer Arbeit, sondern auch in unserem familiären und gesellschaftlichen Leben erfahren, wirbelt uns immer weiter nach außen, weg von unserem Zentrum. Wir haben es zugelassen, an die Oberfläche unseres Lebens geworfen zu werden – wir verwechseln Geschäftigkeit mit Lebendigkeit, doch dieses oberflächliche Dasein ist in sich unbefriedigend.

Eine Wallfahrt bietet uns die Gelegenheit, langsamer zu werden und etwas Weite in unser Leben hineinzulassen. In diesem stilleren Umfeld können wir über die tiefere Bedeutung unseres Lebens nachdenken und über den Grund, wozu wir hierher kamen. Der Camino ermutigt uns, die immerwährende Frage zu stellen – wer bin ich? Und entscheidend ist: er bietet uns Zeit dafür, die Antworten zu verstehen und zu integrieren. Also hetzt nicht auf dem Camino – nimm dir die Zeit, die er erfordert, denn er könnte sich als ein entscheidender Wendepunkt in deinem Leben entpuppen.

Buen camino !

Legenda:

Total km   Distanza totale della tappa indicata

   Adatto al dislivello (100 m verticali = a 0,5 km addizionali)

(850m) **Alto▲**   Curva di dislivello / Punto più elevato di ogni tappa

< Ⓐ Ⓗ >   Alloggio intermezzo (*spesso meno occupato / più basso*)

◀ **3.5**   Distanza esatta tra punti (3,5 km = ± 1'ora di cammino)

─●150m >/^/<   Distanze parziali: a 150 m a destra > / proseguire dritto ^ /
                                               < a sinistra

............/........   Cammino o sentiero (*verde*:cammini naturali /*grigio*:calcestruzzo)

━━○━━   Strada secondaria (*grigio*: asfalto) / Rotonda

━━**N-11**━━   Strada principale [N-] (*rosso*: maggiore traffico e pericolo)

══**A-1**══   Autostrada (*azzurra*: colore abituale)

+++++++●   Via di treno / Stazione

● ● ● ● ●   Itinerario principale (*giallo*: ± 80% dei pellegrini)

● ● ● ● ●   Itinerario scenico (*verde*: più lontana / meno pellegrini)

● ● ● ● ●   Itinerario per strada (*grigio*: più asfalto)

● ● ● ● ●   Giro opzionale a un punto di interesse (*azzurrino*)

X ? ❶   Croce / Punto di Opzione / Attenzione speciale

↑ ⩊ ┋   Mulino di vento / Belvedere / Antenna di radio

·—·/·—·   Frontiera statale / Limiti di provinciali

∼/∼   Fiume / Fiumicello

◯/◯   Lago oppure estuario / Bosco

♱ ♦ ✝   Chiesa / Cappella / Calvario

Ⓕ 🍺 Ⓜ   Fontana di acqua potabile / Caffè bar / Mini-mercato

menú   *V.*   Ristorante *menú de peregrino* / Vegetariano

🅸 🏠 ✕   Turismo / Casa signorile / Picnic

✚ ➕ ✉   Farmacia / Ospedale / Posta

✈ 🚏 ⛽   Aeroporto / Stazione degli autobus / Distributore di benzina

••   XIIthc   Monumento storico / Secolo XII

Ⓐ❶   **Ⓙ**   Ostello (-i) di pellegrino *albergue* / Ostello per la gioventù

Ⓗ Ⓟ Ⓒ   Hotel *H*°–*H*°°°° 30–90 / Pensione *P* €20+ / Casa Rurale Incl.*CR* €35+

Ⓗ Ⓐ Ⓙ   *Alloggio fuori itinerario*

[32]   Numero di posti letto (in genere letti a castello)

[÷4]+   ÷ numero di stanze / + *anche stanze private* €20+

Par.   Ostello parrocchiale *donazione (€5+)*

Conv.   Ostello in un convento o monastero *donazione (€5+)*

Muni.   Ostello municipale €5+

Xunta   Ostello della Xunta di Galizia €6

Asoc.   Ostello di un'associazione €7

Priv. (*)   Ostello privato (Rete di Ostelli*) €10+ / Incl. Compresa la colazione
      I prezzi sono indicativi; ai soli fini comparativi

   Cartina della città

(Pop.–Alt. m)   Popolazione – Altitudine in metri

   Periferia (*grigio*)

   Centro Storico (*marrone*)

Introduzione: Nelle vite di tutti noi c'è un eccesso parafernale. Con la pretensione di alleggerire il carico, abbiamo creato questa sottile edizione con le mappe multilingue. Tutto ciò è stato possibile grazie al lavoro disinteressato delle Associazioni di Pellegrini che hanno segnato il percorso in modo tale che, oggi giorno, soltanto ne abbiamo bisogno della informazione più di base per raggiungere la nostra destinazione. Risulta difficile perdersi se in tutti i momenti rimaniamo concentrati e attenti alle frecce gialle che spuntano verso Santiago e Finisterre: nel raccoglimento c'è la chiave. Prendi un tempo per familiarizzarti con i simboli della mappa che troverai sulla pagina di fronte.

Lo standard e il costo di alloggio pellegrino varia dagli ostelli *Xunta* offrire servizi di base a partire da € 6 (senza prenotazione) prima di ostelli privati a partire da € 10 + ma spesso con servizi aggiuntivi come lavatrici e asciugatrici. Una base pasto di 3 portate con vino *(menú peregrino)* costi circa € 9.

Queste cartine multilingue sono una riconoscimento alla fratellanza internazionale del Cammino. Esso favorisce il sentimento di cameratismo e comunione; un'intenzione spirituale condivisa che giace nel cuore del pellegrinaggio. È questa focalizzazione trascendente quello che distingue il pellegrinaggio dal trekking di lunga distanza.

Tutti percorriamo due cammini simultaneamente: il cammino esteriore, per cui trasciniamo il nostro corpo, e il cammino interiore del anima. Dobbiamo essere consapevoli di tutti e due e prenderci il tempo per preparaci adeguatamente. Il cammino tradizionale di pellegrino è viaggiare s olo, a piedi, portando in carico tutti i possessi materiali di cui ne abbiamo bisogno nel viaggio che abbiamo davanti. Questo offre la prima lezione al pellegrino: lasciare indietro tutto quello superfluo e viaggiare soltanto con quello strettamente necessario. La preparazione per il cammino interiore è simile: incominciamo buttando via la spazzatura psichica accumulata lungo gli anni, come risentimenti, pregiudizi e sistemi di credenze fuori moda. Con una mente e un cuore aperti assimileremo con maggior facilità le lezioni con cui ci troveremo lungo questo Cammino delle verifiche.

È da tanto tempo che siamo addormentati. Pur il caotico mondo che ci gira attorno, o forse a causa di esso, c'è qualcosa che ci scuote affinché svegliamo della nostra amnesia collettiva. Un segnale di questo risveglio è il numero di persone che si sentono attratte per fare i cammini. Il ritmo frenetico della vita moderna, che esperimentiamo non soltanto al lavoro ma anche nella nostra vita famigliare e nella sociale, fa si che ogni volta sfarfalliamo più lontano del nostro centro. Abbiamo consenso di essere lanciati alla superficie delle nostre vite, al confondere essere occupati con essere vivi, ma questa esistenza superficiale risulta intrinsecamente insoddisfacente.

Il pellegrinaggio ci offre l'opportunità di ridurre il ritmo e di dotare le nostre vite di una certa ampiezza. In questo spazio più tranquillo si può riflettere riguardo al significato più profondo delle nostre vite e le ragioni per cui siamo venuti qui. Il Cammino ci anima a farci la domanda perenne: chi sono?. E, quello che risulta cruciale, ci fornisce il tempo per poter capire e assimilare le risposte. Quindi non ti affrettare a percorrere il Cammino: prendi il tempo di cui ne abbia bisogno, perché potrebbe diventare il punto di inflessione della tua vita.

Buen camino !

Légende:

Total km	Distance totale de l'étape
	Distance équivalente avec ajout de la déclivité (100 m vertical =
(850m) **Alto ▲**	Courbes de niveau / Point culminant de l'étape / 0,5 km add.)
< Ⓐ Ⓗ >	Hébergement en cours d'étape (*souvent moins occupé silencieux*)
◄ 3.5	Distance précise entre points (3,5 km = ± 1 heure de marche)
→●150m > / ^ / <	Distances intermédiaires : à 150m tourner à droite> / ^tout droit /
	à gauche>

⸏⸏⸏⸏⸏ / ⸏⸏⸏⸏⸏	Sentier ou piste (*vert* : en terre / *gris*: béton)
━━○━━	Route secondaire (*gris*: asphalte) / Rond-point
━ N-11 ━	Route principale [N]-(*rouge* : circulation plus importante et danger)
━ A-1 ━	Autoroute (*bleu*: couleur conventionnelle)
+++++++●	Voie ferrée / Gare

● ● ● ● ●	Route principale (*jaune*: ± 80% des pèlerins)
● ● ● ● ●	Route panoramique (*vert*: plus à l'écart / moins pèlerins)
● ● ● ● ●	Itinéraire par la route (*gris* : plus d'asphalte)
● ● ● ● ●	Détour facultatif vers un point d'intérêt (*turquoise*)
X **?** **❶**	Carrefour / Point de l'option / Faire particulièrement attention

✝ ⸜⸝ ↑	Moulin à vent / Point de vue / Antenne radio
▪—▪ / ▪—▪	Frontière nationale / limite de province
∼ / ∼	Rivière / Ruisseau
⬭ / ∼	Lac ou estuaire / Forêt
✝ ⸜ ✝	Église / Chapelle / Croix

ⓖ 🍺 🏪	Fontaine d'eau potable / Café-bar / Supérette
menú *V.*	restaurant avec menu du pèlerin / Végétarien
🄸 🏰 ✕	Tourisme / Quinta ou manoir / table de pique-nique
➊ ➕ ✉	Pharmacie / Hôpital / Poste
⊕ 🚌 🅿	Aéroport / Gare routière / Station Service
•• XII[th]c	Site historique / XIIe siècle

Ⓐ❶ **Ⓙ**	Auberge(s) de pèlerins / Auberge de jeunesse / *CR* Incl. 35 € +
Ⓗ **Ⓟ** **Ⓒ**	Hôtel *H°* –*H°°°°* 30–90 € / Pension *P* 20 €+ / Chambre d'hôte
Ⓗ Ⓐ Ⓙ	*Hébergement hors itinéraire*
[32]	Nombre de places-lits (en général superposés)
[÷4]+	÷ nombre de dortoirs + *aussi des chambres privées*
Par.	Auberge de paroisse (don / 5 €)
Conv.	Auberge dans un couvent ou monastère (don / 5 € +)
Muni.	Auberge municipale 5 €
Xunta	Auberge du gouvernement *Xunta de Galicia* € 6
Asoc.	Auberge d'association € 7 / Incl. petit déjeuner compris
Priv. (*)	Auberge privée (réseau des auberges*) 10 € + / Incl.
	Tous les prix sont approximatifs; à des fins de comparaison
▭	Plan de ville
(Pop.–Alt. m)	Population - Altitude en mètres
▬	Banlieue (gris)
◰	Centre historique centro histórico (brun)

Introduction : Dans la vie de chacun de nous, il y a trop d'objets matériels. Dans le but d'alléger cette charge, nous avons créé une édition légère avec des cartes multilingues. Cela a été possible grâce au travail désintéressé des associations de pèlerins qui ont si bien marqué le parcours qu'aujourd'hui, pour atteindre la destination, on a simplement besoin de renseignements de base. Il est difficile de se perdre si on reste à tout moment concentré et attentif aux flèches jaunes indiquant Santiago et Finisterre : la clé, c'est la concentration. Prenez le temps de vous familiariser avec les symboles sur la page opposée.

La norme et le coût de l'hébergement pèlerin varie d'auberges *Xunta* offrant des installations de base de 6 € (pas de réservation) à auberges privées à partir de € 10 + mais souvent avec des équipements supplémentaires tels que machines à laver et sécher. Une base repas de 3 plats avec du vin (Menú peregrino) coûte environ € 9

Ces cartes multilingues témoignent de la solidarité internationale du *Camino* qui favorise un sentiment de camaraderie et de fraternité, et d'une démarche spirituelle partagée qui est au cœur du pèlerinage. C'est ce qui distingue le pèlerinage de la grande randonnée.

Nous avançons tous en même temps sur deux voies : la voie externe, pour laquelle nous entrainons notre corps, et la voie interne qui correspond au voyage intérieur de l'âme. Nous devons être conscients de ces deux voies et prendre le temps de bien nous préparer. La tradition veut que le pèlerin chemine tout seul, à pied, portant ce qui lui est nécessaire pour le voyage. C'est la première leçon du pèlerin : laisser derrière soi tout le superflu et voyager avec seulement ce qui est nécessaire. La préparation pour le chemin interne est similaire : nous commençons par nous débarrasser des scories psychiques accumulées au fil des ans, comme les ressentiments, les préjugés et les systèmes de croyance dépassés. Avec un esprit et un cœur plus ouverts, on peut plus facilement assimiler les leçons que l'on tire le long de cette très ancienne voie de découverte.

Longtemps nous sommes restés endormis. Malgré le monde chaotique qui nous entoure, ou peut-être à cause de lui, il y a quelque chose qui nous travaille, et nous nous réveillons alors de notre amnésie collective. Un signe de cet éveil est le nombre de personnes qui sont attirées par les pèlerinages. Le rythme effréné de la vie moderne dont nous faisons l'expérience non seulement au travail, mais aussi dans notre vie familiale et sociale, nous propulse plus loin de notre centre. Nous nous sommes laissés projeter sur la surface de nos vies, en confondant celle-ci avec l'hyperactivité, mais cette existence superficielle n'est pas intrinsèquement satisfaisante.

Le pèlerinage nous donne l'occasion de ralentir le rythme et de donner une respiration à nos vies. Dans cet espace silencieux, on peut réfléchir sur le sens profond de notre existence et sur les raisons de notre présence sur terre. Le *Camino* nous incite à nous poser l'éternelle question : qui suis-je ? Et il nous donne le temps – ce qui est crucial – de comprendre et d'assimiler les réponses. Alors ne vous précipitez pas pour parcourir la route : prenez le temps nécessaire, car c'est peut-être le tournant de votre vie.

Quelle que soit la voie que vous choisissez, votre destination finale est la même. Le seul choix que vous ayez est le temps que vous prenez pour l'atteindre.

Buen camino !

Explicação das legendas dos mapas:

Total km	Distância total da etapa
⛰	Ajustado para subida (100 m na vertical = mais 0,5 km)
(850m)**Alto▲**	Linha de relevo / Ponto mais alto da etapa
< Ⓐ Ⓗ >	Alojamento intermédio
◄ 3.5	Distância exacta entre pontos (3.5 km = ± 1 hora andar)
—●150m >/^/<	Distâncias intermédias 150 metros virar à direita>
	/ seguir em frente^ / <virar à esquerda
⅏⅏⅏⅏/⅏⅏⅏	Caminho ou carreiro (*verde*: caminho rural / *cinzento*: concreto)
══o══	Estrada secundária (*cinzento*: asfalto) / Rotunda
N-11	Estrada principal (*vermelho*: mais trânsito e perigo)
A-1	Auto-estrada (*azul*: cor convencional das auto-estradas)
++++++●	Linha de trem / Estação ferroviária
● ● ● ● ●	Percurso principal (*amarelo*: ± 80% de todos os peregrinos)
● ● ● ● ●	Percurso rural alternativo (*verde*: mais afastado/menos peregrinos)
● ● ● ● ●	Desvio opcional para ponto de interesse (*turquesa*)
● ● ● ● ●	Percurso alternativo (*cinzento*: mais estradas – asfalto)
X ? ⓘ	Cruzamento / Opção / Muito cuidado
↑ ⚕ ⍓	Miradouro / Moinho/ Antena de transmissão
·—·/·—·	Fronteira nacional / Limite de província
∼/∼	Rio / Ribeiro
◯/◯	Estuário marítimo ou fluvial / Área florestal
⛪ ⍋ ✝	Igreja / Capela / Cruzeiro
Ⓕ ☕ ⍰	Fonte / Café-bar / Mini-mercado
menú *V.*	Menu peregrino ±€9 / *V. V*egetariano
ⓘ ⌂ ✗	Posto de turismo / Solar / Picnic
✚ ✚ ✉	Hospital / Farmácia / Posto de correios
✈ ◻ ⛽	Aeroporto / Estação autocarros / Bomba gasolina
⠿ XIIᵗʰc	Monumento histórico / Século 12
Ⓐ❶ Ⓙ	Albergue(s) de peregrinos / Pousada de juventude
Ⓗ Ⓟ Ⓒ	Hotel *H*°–*H*°°°° €30–90 / Pensão *P* €20+ / Casa rural *CR* €35+
Ⓗ Ⓐ Ⓙ	*alojamento perto mas fora*
[32]	Número de lugares (geralmente beliches)
[÷4]+	÷ numero de dormitórios + *quartos particulares*
Par.	Albergue parroquial doação / €5
Conv.	Albergue en un convento o monasterio doação / €5+
Muni.	Albergue municipal €5+
Xunta	Albergue de la Xunta de Galicia €6
Asoc.	Albergue a associação €7+
Priv. (*)	Alojamento privado (*Rede de Albergues) €10–15
	Os preços são aproximados e apenas a título de comparação.
▭	Planta da cidade
(Pop.–Alt. m)	População - altitude, em metros
▭	Subúrbios (*cinzento*)
▭	Centro histórico (*castanho*)

Introdução: Todos carregamos demasiados acessórios nas nossas vidas – num esforço para aliviar o peso produzimos este leve e fino volume com mapas multilingues. Isto foi possível devido ao trabalho altruísta de organizações de apoio aos peregrinos que sinalizaram o Caminho de modo a que, hoje em dia, necessitemos de um mínimo de informações para nos levar ao destino. Será difícil perdermo-nos se nos mantivermos atentos às setas amarelas que indicam o caminho até Santiago e Finisterre - o estado de alerta é a chave. Tire um tempo para se familiarizar com o símbolos do mapa oposto.

O padrão e custo de alojamento peregrino varia de albergues *xunta* oferecendo facilidades básicas de 6 € (sem reserva prévia) para albergues privados a partir de € 10 +, mas geralmente com recursos adicionais, tais como máquinas de lavar e secar secadora. O último um benefício real em tempo de chuva. A 3 prato principal refeição básica com vinho (menú peregrino) a partir de 9 €.

Estes mapas multilingues reconhecem a irmandade internacional do Caminho. Espera-se que ajudem a forjar um sentido de camaradagem e comunhão – a partilha de uma intenção comum que está na base da peregrinação. É este objectivo transcendente que distingue uma peregrinação de uma mera caminhada.

Todos percorremos dois caminhos simultaneamente – o caminho exterior ao longo do qual transportamos o nosso corpo e um caminho interior, da alma. Devemos estar conscientes de ambos e encontrar o tempo de preparação adequada. A maneira tradicional do peregrino é viajar sozinho, a pé, carregando todas as possessões materiais necessárias para a viagem que tem pela frente. Isto proporciona a primeira lição do peregrino – deixar para trás tudo o que é supérfluo e viajar com o que é realmente necessário. A preparação para o caminho interior é semelhante – devemos começar por abandonar o lixo psíquico acumulado ao longo dos anos, os ressentimentos, os preconceitos e as crenças antiquadas. Com uma mente aberta poderemos assimilar mais facilmente as lições a tirar ao longo deste Caminho de Busca.

Há muito tempo que andamos adormecidos. Apesar do mundo caótico à nossa volta ou talvez por isso, algo está a compelir-nos para o despertar da nossa amnésia colectiva. Um sinal deste despertar é o número de pessoas atraídas pelo Caminho. O ritmo agitado da vida moderna, que sentimos tanto no nosso trabalho como na nossa vida familiar e social, atira-nos para longe de nós próprios. Deixámo-nos afastar para a periferia da nossa vida confundindo estar ocupado com estar vivo, mas esta existência superficial acaba por ser inerentemente insatisfatória.

A peregrinação oferece uma oportunidade de abrandar e dar amplitude à nossa vida. É nesse espaço mais calmo que se torna possível reflectir no significado mais profundo das nossas vidas e nas razões porque estamos aqui. O Caminho encoraja-nos a fazer a pergunta essencial – quem sou eu? E fundamentalmente dá-nos tempo para que as respostas sejam compreendidas e absorvidas. Portanto não apresse o Caminho – leve o tempo que precisar, ele pode-se tornar um ponto essencial de mudança na sua vida.

Buen camino...

Kaartsymbolen in deze handleiding:

Total km Totale afstand voor het aangegeven traject
 Gecorrigeerd voor de klim (100m verticaal=0,5 km extra)
(850m) **Alto▲** Contouren / Hoogste punt van elk traject
< Ⓐ Ⓗ > Accommodaties onderweg (*vaak minder druk / stiller*)
◀ **3.5** Exacte afstand tussen twee punten(3,5 km= ongeveer 1uur wandelen)
–●150m >/ ^ /< Onderlinge afstand 150m rechts> / s/o recht door/ links<

ıιιιιιιιιιι /ıιιιιιιι Pad of spoor (*groen*: onverharde paden / *grijs*: verharde weg)
━━○━━ Secundaire weg (*grijs*: asfalt) / Rotonde
━ **N-11** ━ Hoofd(N-)weg (*rood*: extra verkeer en gevaar)
══ **A-1** ══ Autosnelweg (*blauw*: conventionele kleur)
+++++++● Spoorweg / Station

● ● ● ● ● Hoofdweg (*geel*: ong. 80% van de pelgrims)
● ● ● ● ● Schilderachtige route (*groen*: meer afgelegen / minder pelgrims)
● ● ● ● ● Verharde weg (*grijs*: meer asfalt)
● ● ● ● ● Optionele omweg desvio naar bezienswaardigheid (*turqoise*)
X ❓ ❶ kruispunt / Optie / Extra oppassen

↑ ⁖ ⁜ Windmolen / Uitkijkpunt / Zendmast
·━·/·━· Nationale grens / Provinciale grens
∼ / ∼ Rivier / Beek
◯ / ◯ Zee- of riviermonding / Bos
✝ ⁑ ✝ Kerk / Kapel / Kruisbeeld langs de weg

Ⓕ 🍺 ♨ Drinkwater / Café bar / kleine markt
menú *V.* Restaurant *menú peregrino* / Vegetarisch
🛈 🏠 ✕ Tourisme / Landhuis / Picknicktafel
✚ ✚ ✉ Apotheek / Ziekenhuis / Postkantoor
⊕ 🚌 ⛽ Vliegveld / Bus station / Tankstation
•• XII[th]c Oud monument / 12th eeuw

Ⓐ❶ Ⓙ Pelgrim hostel(s) / Jeugdherberg
Ⓗ Ⓟ Ⓒ Hotel *H-H*****€30-90 / Pension *P**€20+ / B&B *CR* €35+ Incl.
Ⓗ Ⓐ Ⓙ *accommodaties buiten de route*
[32] Aantal slaapplaatsen (meestal stapelbedden)
[÷4]+ + aantal slaapzalen + ook privé kamers
Par. Kerk Parochie hostel Parroquia schenking *donativo* / €5
Conv. Convent of klooster hostel schenking *donativo* / €5
Muni. Gemeentelijk hostel €5+
Xunta Galician overheid Xunta de Galicia hostel €6
Asoc. Vereniging hostel €7+
Priv. (*) Particulier hostel (netwerk*) €10+ / Incl. inclusief ontbijt
 Alle prijzen bij benadering; alleen voor vergelijkbare doeleinden
 Stadsplattegrond
(Pop.–Alt. m) (pop.—Alt.m) Inwoners-hoogte in meters
 Voorsteden (*grijs*)
 Historisch centrum centro historico (*bruin*)

Introductie: Ieder van ons heeft te veel ballast in zijn leven – in een poging om de last te verlichten, hebben wij een compacte uitgave van gidsen geproduceerd met meertalige kaarten. Dit is mogelijk gemaakt door het onbaatzuchtige werk van pegrimsverenigingen die de route dusdanig gemarkeerd hebben, dat wij slechts zeer beperkt aanvullende informatie nodig hebben om onze bestemming te bereiken. Het zal moeilijk zijn om te verdwalen wanneer we aanwezig blijven in elk moment en aandachtig letten op de gele pijlen die de weg wijzen naar Santiago en Finisterre – bewuste aandacht is de sleutel. Neem de tijd om vertrouwd te raken met de kaartsymbolen op de pagina hiernaast.

De kwaliteit en kosten van pelgrim accommodaties variëren van parochie hostels op basis van donaties, gemeentelijke hostels die basis faciliteiten aanbieden voor € 6,00 (niet van tevoren te boeken) tot particuliere hostels vanaf €10,00 die over het algemeen extra faciliteiten bieden zoals wasmachines en drogers *secadora*. Dit laatste is een echte zegen bij regenachtig weer. Een standaard driegangenmenu met wijn is beschikbaar, *menú peregrino*, vanaf € 9,00.

Door deze meertalige gidsen herken je de internationale gemeenschap van de camino. Dit kan bijdragen aan een gevoel van samenhorigheid en kameraadschap; een gedeelde spirituele intentie die ten grondslag ligt aan de pelgrimage. Het is deze alle overstijgende intentie die de pelgrimage onderscheidt van een gewone langeafstandswandeling.

Ieder van ons bewandelt twee paden tegelijkertijd: de route die we fysiek bewandelen en het innerlijke pad van de ziel. We moeten aandacht hebben voor beiden en onszelf dienovereenkomstig voorbereiden. De traditionele manier van de pelgrim is alleen te reizen, te voet, met in je rugzak alleen die benodigdheden die je denkt nodig te hebben voor je reis. Dit biedt de eerste les voor de pelgrim – om al het overbodige achter te laten en alleen het hoogst noodzakelijke mee te nemen. Voorbereiding voor het innerlijke pad is vergelijkbaar – we beginnen bij het loslaten van psychische ballast die we in de jaren verzameld hebben, zoals ergernissen, vooroordelen en achterhaalde overtuigingen. Met een open geest en een open hart zullen we de lessen die geleerd kunnen worden langs het oude Spirituele Pad makkelijker in ons op kunnen nemen.

We zijn lange tijd in slaap gedut. Ondanks de chaotische wereld om ons heen, of misschien juist daardoor, heeft iets ons wakker geschud uit onze collectief geheugenverlies. Een teken van dit ontwaken is het aantal mensen dat zich aangetrokken voelt om de caminos te bewandelen. Het hectische tempo van het moderne leven, niet alleen ervaren in ons werk maar ook in ons gezins- en sociale leven, brengt ons verder weg van onze kern. We hebben onszelf toegestaan om oppervlakkig door het leven te gaan – daarbij drukte verwarrend met levendigheid, maar dit oppervlakkige bestaan is onvermijdelijk onbevredigend.

Pelgrimage biedt ons de mogelijkheid om te vertragen en wat ruimte toe te laten in ons leven. In deze stillere ruimte kunnen we reflecteren op de diepere betekenis van ons leven en de redenen van ons bestaan. De camino spoort ons aan om ons de eeuwige vraag te stellen – Wie ben ik? En cruciaal, het geeft ons tijd om de antwoorden te begrijpen en te integreren. Dus haast je niet op de camino – neem de tijd die het nodig heeft want het zou zomaar het cruciale keerpunt in je leven kunnen zijn.

Welke route we ook nemen, onze uiteindelijke bestemming staat vast. De enige keuze die we hebben is hoe lang we erover doen om te arriveren.

Buen camino...

Legenda do mapy używanej w tym przewodniku:

Total km — Całkowita odległość na mapie etapów

Dostosowanie do podejść (100 m w pionie=dodatkowe 0,5 km)

(850m) **Alto** ▲ — Profile / Najwyższy punkt każdego etapu

< A 🏠 > — Noclegi pośrednia (często mniej zajęty / ciszej)

◄ 3.5 — Dokładna odległość między punktami (3,5 km = ± 1 godz.)

●150m > / ^ / < — Odległości pośrednie •150 m skręt w prawo> / prosto^ /
< w lewo

░░░░░ / ░░░░░ — Ścieżka lub szlak (*zielony*: ścieżka naturalna / *szary*: betonowa)

═══○═══ — Droga podrzędna (*szary*: asfalt) / Rondo

═══**N-11**═══ — Droga główna [N-] Nacional (*czerwony*: wzmożony ruch)

═══**A-1**═══ — Autostrada (*niebieski*: zwykłe autostrady)

++++++● — Kolej ferrocarril / stacja estación

● ● ● ● ● — Trasa główna (*żółty*: ± 80% pielgrzymów)

● ● ● ● ● — Trasa krajobrazowa (*zielony*: dłuższa / mniej pielgrzymów)

● ● ● ● ● — Droga alternatywna (*szary*: więcej asfaltu)

● ● ● ● ● — Szlak alternatywny (*turkusowy*) do interesujących miejsc

X ❓ ❶ — Skrzyżowanie *cruce* / Opcja *opción* / uwaga! *¡cuidado!*

🌀 ☀ ☖ — Wiatrak / Punkt widokowy / Maszt radiowy

▪━▪/▪━▪ — Granica państwa / Granica prowincji

〜/〜 — Rzeka / Potok

◯/◯ — Morze lub jezioro / Obszar leśny

✝ ♟ ✝ — Kościół / kapliczka / Krzyż przydrożny

🅖 ☕ ♨ — Źródło z wodą pitną / Kawiarnia / Sklep

menú **V.** — Menú peregrino obiad z trzech dań i wino / V. wegetariański

ℹ 🏯 ✕ — Informacja turystyczna / Dwór / Miejsce piknikowe

✚ ✚ ✉ — Apteka / Szpital / Poczta

✈ 🚏 ⛽ — Lotnisko / Dworzec autobusowy / Stacja benzynowa

• • XIIth c — Zabytek / XII w.

🅐❶ 🅙 — Schronisko dla pielgrzymów / Schronisko młodzieżowe

🅗 🅟 🅒 — Hotel *H-H*****€30-90 / Pensjonat *P** €20+ / B&B *CR* €35+

🅗 🅐 🅙 — (zakwaterowanie poza trasą)

[32] — Liczba łóżek (zwykle łóżka piętrowe)

[÷4]+ — ÷ Liczba pokoi / + dodatkowe pokoje prywatne €20+

Par. — Ofiara za nocleg w parafii / €5

Conv. — Ofiara za nocleg w klasztorze / €5

Muni. — Schronisko miejskie €5+

Xunta — Schronisko należące do regionu Galicji *(Xunta hostel)* €6

Asoc. — Schronisko prowadzone przez stowarzyszenie €7+

Priv. (*) — Schronisko prywatne (sieciowe*) €10+ / ze śniadaniem
Ceny podane są orientacyjnie; tylko dla porównania

☐ — Plan miasta z numerem strony

(Pop.–Alt. m) — Ludność miasta i położenie n.p.m. (w metrach)

☐ — Przedmieścia *(szary)*

☐ — Historyczne centrum *(brązowy)*

Wstęp: Wszyscy posiadamy zbyt dużo rzeczy: aby ulżyć w drodze, wydaliśmy ten skromny zbiór map.

Było to możliwe dzięki bezinteresownej pracy stowarzyszeń pielgrzymów, które oznakowały szlaki tak, że obecnie potrzebujemy jedynie podstawowych informacji, aby dostać się do naszego celu. Byłoby to trudne, gdybyśmy stale wytężali uwagę na znalezienie wszystkich żółtych strzałek oznaczających drogę do Santiago – grunt to skupienie. Zapoznajcie się teraz z symbolami wykorzystanymi na mapach.

Wielojęzyczne mapy dowodzą istnienia międzynarodowej wspólnoty na Camino. Pomaga to rozwijać poczucie wspólnoty i braterstwa, budować wspólnotę duchową, która jest sercem pielgrzymowania. Ów niezwykły ogień odróżnia pątnika od turysty. Zalecamy zakup przewodnika ze wskazówkami, jak najlepiej przygotować się do takiej długiej wyprawy, jednego z polskich lub w poradnik *A Pilgrim's Guide to the Camino Francés.*

Wszyscy wędrujemy równocześnie dwiema ścieżkami: zewnętrzną, którą podąża nasze ciało i wewnętrzną drogą duszy. Trzeba być świadomym obydwu z nich i poświęcić czas na odpowiednie przygotowanie się. Tradycyjnym sposobem pielgrzymowania jest samotna wędrówka piesza i noszenie wszystkiego, czego potrzebujemy w drodze. To pierwsza lekcja dla pątnika: zostawić za sobą wszystko, co zbędne i podróżować jedynie z najbardziej potrzebnym wyposażeniem. Przygotowanie ścieżki wewnętrznej jest podobne: zaczynamy od pozostawienia wszelkich wewnętrznych „nieużytków" nagromadzonych przez lata, jak urazy, uprzedzenia i schematy myślowe. Otwartym umysłem i sercem łatwiej przyswoimy lekcje, które odnajdziemy na tej starej Drodze Doświadczenia.

Przez długi czas byliśmy pogrążeni w drzemce. Pomimo chaosu w otaczającym świecie albo raczej z jego powodu coś nas porusza, aby obudzić się z zapomnienia. Znakiem tego przebudzenia jest liczba ludzi, którzy są pociągani do wędrówki przez Camino. Pospieszne życie nowoczesnego świata nie tylko w naszej pracy, ale też w rodzinie i społeczeństwie, prowadzi nas na zewnątrz i pozostawia z dala od naszego wnętrza. Pozwoliliśmy się wyrzucić na powierzchnię naszego życia - myląc "bycie zajętym" z "byciem żywym". Ale ta powierzchowna egzystencja wcale nas nie cieszy.

Pielgrzymowanie daje okazję do tego, aby zwolnić i aby dać naszemu życiu trochę przestrzeni. W tej spokojniejszej przestrzeni możemy zastanowić się nad głębszym znaczeniem naszego życia i nad tym, po co istniejemy. Camino daje nam odwagę do zadawania nieprzemijających pytań: kim jestem? Oraz daje czas na odkrycie i zrozumienie odpowiedzi. A więc nie spieszcie się na Camino – dajcie sobie czas, jakiego wymaga, gdyż może stanowić punkt zwrotny w waszym życiu.

Którąkolwiek drogę wybierzemy, nasze ostateczne miejsce przeznaczenia jest pewne. Jedyny wybór, jakiego mamy dokonać, to czas, którego nam potrzeba, aby dotrzeć na *buen camino*.

Santiago de Compostela

Compostelana

Fisterana

Cabo de Finisterre

Muxía

Muxianna

All routes remain largely unchanged since the first guidebook were published in 2001. Nature has healed much of the damage caused by forest fires that devastated whole tracts of eucalyptus and pine forest and the coast has largely recovered from the effects of the Prestige oil disaster which spawned the ecological movement in Galicia 'Never Again' *Nunca Maís*.

The biggest change is still the increasing number of pilgrims drawn to experience the caminos. During the past decade the number of pilgrims commencing their journey in Sarria has increased from 39,583 to 58,554. Similar statistics for pilgrims arriving in Santiago *from* Finisterre are only available from 2011 when this latter route was first officially recognised. That year 72 pilgrims collected a compostela increasing to 652 in 2014. But these figures don't tell the whole story because the vast majority found walking the route to the coast at Finisterre are seasoned pilgrims who have no need to collect an additional 'certificate' upon which the above statistics are based. *La Voz de Galicia* estimated 45,000 pilgrims visited Finisterre during the Holy Year in 2011 but the majority will have arrived by bus.

A synopsis of the history, legends and myths surrounding this fascinating corner at the 'End of the World' *Finis Terra* are included as a backdrop for those interested in their exploration. However, it is their symbolism and the mystical experience to which they point that really matters. Literalism can be a hindrance to a deeper understanding of our lives and our place in the Cosmos. The question is not whether the earthly remains of St. James lie buried in Santiago nor whether Jesus travelled to Finisterre to meet the Druidic masters there – what really matters is whether we can absorb and live out the truth of their core teaching of unconditional love and forgiveness. That is the real task of the true initiate on the spiritual path through this earthly life.

For the majority of pilgrims commencing their journey in Sarria, Santiago is their final destination and they simply aren't aware of – or haven't thought about continuing to Finisterre or Muxía. Others are caught within a tightening schedule requiring an early return home. Some squeeze in a visit by bus but this is no substitute for walking the path which remains one of the most significant of the many camino itineraries. The paths to Finisterre and Muxía provide an opportunity to integrate our camino experiences before we find ourselves back home... in the fast lane.

In the event that you have already walked to Santiago from Sarria or along one of the myriad routes that converge on this fabled city, you will doubtless be lean and travelling light. Your experiences will stand you well for the journey ahead. Finisterre will challenge but not disappoint. While the bones of the great Saint may lie in Santiago, his spirit flourishes along the Royal Way *Camiño Real* and provides the inspiration and energy to keep on going. Finisterre may prove a humbling experience after the relative glamour of Santiago. If, on the other hand, you are setting off from Santiago on this circuit as a 'novice' pilgrim you may wish to check out advice on preparation. The companion guide *Camino de Santiago (Camino Francés)* has detailed suggestions on what to bring and, just as importantly, on what to leave behind.

Pilgrimage is experienced on many different levels. At one end is the physical challenge of walking a long distance route in the minimum time with a group of friends. How deep we choose to make the experience is, of course, up to us but perhaps now is an opportunity to experience pilgrimage at a pace that allows for the inner alchemy of introspection. The extended periods of silence will allow time for reflection and to integrate insights leading to change and growth. It is in the silence that we will most likely encounter our *Self* and that may prove a pivotal turning point.

While there is a plethora of guidebooks on the routes to Santiago there is a dearth of information on the path to Finisterre and Muxía. Perhaps it is Finisterre's connection with its pagan past that has acted as a deterrent. This mysterious headland marked the fault line between a Christian point of reference to the east and a pagan orientation to the west. The rising sun over *Monte Pindo* flooded through the entrance door to the Christian hermitage of San Guillerme but its setting over the western horizon to the Land of Eternal Youth *Tir-na-nóg* was watched over by the pagan Altar to the Sun *Ara Solis*. In the medieval period the focus within Spain was narrowed on Santiago de Compostela but to the wider world that focus had always been westward. That is why references to Finisterre come to us from foreign travellers and historians, from Ptolemy of Egypt at the dawn of the Christian era to George Borrow from England in the 18th century.

Whatever the reason for its relative obscurity, the fact remains that only a small band of pilgrims who make it to Santiago choose to walk on to the coast. But the popularity of this route is on the increase boosted not only by those drawn to walk *to* Finisterre but by those inspired to walk *back* to Santiago. Finisterre and Muxía now form starting points for pilgrims going to Santiago. As the routes are over 100 km it allows the bona fide pilgrim to apply for a compostela.

Finisterre now acts as both destination and starting point. However, if you are drawn to quieter reflection you might be advised to continue along the remote pathway to Muxía. While it is a thriving fishing port it has a quiet unhurried air and is sufficiently far enough off the beaten track to offer space to integrate the camino experience. It is thus an ideal place in which to write up our diaries and re-orientate and re-dedicate our Selves towards the spiritual reality underpinning our lives before we head back to consensus reality and the hectic 'realism' of unconscious materialism and its never-ending dramas.

Whichever path you take – travel well fellow pilgrim and may you find and become *the peace of God that passes all understanding*.

Preparation – A Quick Guide:

[1] Practical Considerations:

• **When?** Spring is often wet and windy but the route is relatively quiet with early flowers appearing. Summer is busy and hot and hostels often full. Autumn usually provides the most stable weather with harvesting adding to the colour and celebrations of the countryside. Winter is solitary and cold with reduced daylight hours for walking and many hostels will be closed.

• **How long?** Sarria to Santiago is 115 km and divided into 5 stages corresponding to an average daily walk of 23 km. The entire Finisterre Muxía 'circuit' is 200 km and fits into a more demanding 7 stages with an average 28 km per day. Interim hostels allow the time taken to be varied according to differing abilities and pace.

[2] Preparation – Outer: what do I need to take *and* leave behind.

• Buy your boots in time to walk them in before you go.
• Pack a Poncho – Galicia is notorious for its downpours.
• Bring a hat – sunstroke is painful and can be dangerous.
• Look again if your backpack weighs more than 10 kilos.

What *not* to bring:

• Get rid of all books (except this one – all the maps you need are included.)
• Don't take 'extras', Galicia has shops if you need to replace something.
• If you want to deepen your experience, leave behind:
  – your *camera* – you'll be able to live for the moment rather than memories
  – your *watch* – you'll be surprised how quickly you adapt to a natural clock.
  – your *mobile phone* – break the dependency (excepting solo pilgrims travelling in the winter months when a phone may be useful and a compass necessary to navigate especially in snow when waymarks may become obliterated).

[3] Language learn it now, *before* you go.

[4] Pilgrim Passport, Protocol & Prayer

• Get a *credencial* from your local confraternity – and join it.
• Have consideration for your fellow pilgrims and gratitude for your hosts.
• "May every step be a prayer for peace and leave footprints of loving kindness."

[5] Preparation – Inner: why am I doing this?

Take time to prepare a purpose for this pilgrimage and to complete the self-assessment questionnaire on the next page. Start from the basis that you are essentially a spiritual being on a human journey, not a human being on a spiritual one. We came to learn some lesson and this pilgrimage affords an opportunity to find out what that is. Ask for help and expect it – it's there, now, waiting for you.

SELF-ASSESSMENT *INNER WAYMARKS*

This self-assessment questionnaire is designed to encourage you to reflect on your life and its direction. View it as a snapshot of this moment in your evolving life-story. In the busyness that surrounds us we often fail to take stock of where we are headed. We are the authors of our unfolding drama and we can rewrite the script anytime we choose. Our next steps are up to us...

You might find it useful to initially answer these questions in quick succession as this may allow a more intuitive response. Afterwards, you can reflect more deeply and check if your intellectual answers confirm these, change them or bring in other insights. Download copies of the questionnaire from the *Camino Guides* website – make extra copies so you can repeat the exercise on your return and again in (say) 6 months time. This way we can compare results and ensure we follow through on any insights and commitments that come to us while walking the camino.

❐ How do you differentiate pilgrimage from a long distance walk?

❐ How do you define spirituality – what does it mean to you?

❐ How is your spirituality expressed at home and at work?

❐ What do you see as the primary purpose of your life?

❐ Are you working consciously towards fulfilling that purpose?

❐ How clear are you on your goal and the right direction for you at this time?

❐ How will you recognise resistance to any changes required to reach that goal?

❐ When did you first become aware of a desire to take time-out?

❐ What prompted you originally to go on the camino de Santiago?

❐ Did the prompt come from something that you felt needed changing?

❐ Make a list of what appears to be blocking any change from happening.

❐ What help might you need on a practical, emotional and spiritual level?

❐ How will you recognise the right help or correct answer?

❐ What are the likely challenges in working towards your unique potential?

❐ What are your next steps towards fulfilling that potential?

How aware are you of the following? Score yourself on a level of 1 – 10 and compare these scores again on your return from the camino.

❐ Awareness of your inner spiritual world

❐ Clarity on what inspires you and the capacity to live your passion

❐ Confidence to follow your intuitive sense of the 'right' direction

❐ Ability to recognise your resistance and patterns of defence

❐ Ease with asking for and receiving support from others

REFLECTIONS:

"I am doing the camino once again, looking for something I left behind or perhaps never found. It's like coming home." Notes from a pilgrim from New Mexico recorded in the Pilgrim book in Roncesvalles on the first stage of the journey. What are your reflections for this day?

_____

_____

_____

_____

_____

_____

_____

_____

_____

_____

_____

_____

_____

_____

_____

_____

_____

_____

_____

_____

_____

_____

_____

_____

_____

_____

_____

_____

_____

Map Legend: Once you are familiar with the map symbols you should be able to easily find your way. Unlike conventional maps you always follow in the direction of the page so that everything appears automatically on your left or right. Contour guides are also shown for each day's walk. This will give you an impression of the day's terrain and help you prepare for the uphill stretches and anticipate the downhill ones. They are drawn to an exaggerated scale for emphasis. In addition to actual distance an *adjusted* distance is also provided based on the cumulative height climbed during each stage. This equates to the additional effort and time necessary to walk the stage over and above that required if it were purely a level walk. Remember that your normal walking pace (an average is 1 km in 20 minutes or 3 kph) will decrease, often substantially, towards the end of a hard day's walk.

Abbreviations: s/o = straight on / c. = circa (about) / adj. = adjacent / incl. = inclusive / imm. = immediately / para. = parallel

Waymarks: From Sarria to Santiago it is difficult to get lost as waymarking is obvious and there is generally a line of pilgrims ahead. Thanks to the efforts of the Galician associations waymarking along the more remote paths to Finisterre and Muxía are much improved but there are relatively few other pilgrims to follow and while hopefully you have enough *Castellano* (perhaps *Galego?*) to be able to converse with the rural community you will need to be careful when asking directions as locals are not generally familiar with the waymarked paths through the woods but will direct you along the public roads. Optional routes are also shown which can provide a more reflective path along 'the path less travelled'. The criteria is to minimise the amount of time spent on asphalt which is so hard and tiring underfoot. Finding your way is complicated by the fact that the route has been altered many times over the years and is now waymarked in both directions – stay focused!

Sun Compass: this is provided on each map as an aid to orientation. Even in poor weather we can generally tell the direction of the sun so, for example, if you are travelling from Finisterre to Muxía the route is mostly due north. Early in the morning the sun will be in the east and therefore on your right-hand side. If you suddenly find yourself walking with the sun on your left – stop and make sure you are not following arrows *back* to Finisterre! At midday the sun will be at your back so, likewise, if the sun is in your face – stop and re-assess. You can also use this compass as an aid to understanding the human egoic tendency to identity ourselves as being at the centre of the universe. We say that the sun rises in the east

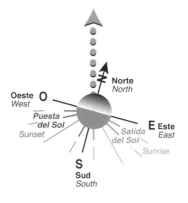

este because that is our experience but of course it is the earth turning on its axis that turns us towards the sun in the morning and away from it at night. This is more than mere semantics – the very thought used to be a heresy punishable by death as Galileo was also to discover. To understand why Finisterre is at the centre of the Santiago story we need to realise the vital importance of the sun and its orientation to ancient civilisations – not only its veneration as the source of life and regeneration with the rising sun *salida del sol* but its symbol of death and resurrection through the setting sun *puesta del sol* in the West *Oeste*.

Each day's stage is measured from the front door of one albergue to the next (or to the Cathedral front door in the case of Santiago). Intermediate hotels or hostels are also shown, those directly on the route in a solid panel and those *off* route with a border only. The number of available beds is also shown [in brackets]. The maps show relevant information only and are therefore not strictly to scale – instead accurate distances are given between each point and this corresponds to the text for ease of reference. The maps are one-directional from Sarria *to* Santiago; if you intend to walk 'in reverse' source conventional maps.

Text and place names are shown as they appear 'on the ground' which is generally in Galician language *Galego* but sometimes appear in Spanish *Castellano*. The Church of St. John may, therefore, appear as *Igrexa San Xoán* or *Igreja San Juan*. Villages in Galicia, tend to straggle without any defined centre and even the local church is frequently located outside the actual town. Distances are measured to an albergue or other clearly defined feature.

Pilgrim Passport *Credencial*: All official pilgrim hostels are reserved exclusively for pilgrims on the camino who must have a pilgrim passport *credencial* that has been stamped along the way. To apply for a *Compostelana* you need to collect 2 stamps each day on your credencial. This second stamp requirement was recently introduced in an effort to eliminate tourists whose main intention was to collect a certificate rather than *bona fide* pilgrims embarking on a spiritual journey. Stamps *sellos* are readily available from churches, hostels, hotels, even bars. These passports are available from your local confraternity and you are encouraged to join and support the largely voluntary work of these organisations (see list of addresses at the back). Apply in good time although some now provide an internet application which speeds processing. Credenciales are available in Sarria and Santiago and need to be presented in order to apply for a Compostelana, Fisterrana or Muxianna

Costs: Xunta hostels have a fixed price €6 per night. If the hostels are full **alternative accommodation** is generally available in hoteles, pensiónes or a type of up-market B&B known as a *casa rural* literally 'rural house' generally built in the traditional Galician style but relatively expensive (€35 - €70 depending on the season). Allow a basic €25–€35 a day to include overnight stay at a Xunta hostel and remainder for food and drink. Some hostels provide a communal dinner (dependent on the warden *hospitalero*) and most have a basic kitchen *cocina* where a meal can be prepared. Alternatively most locations have one or more restaurants to choose from. Pilgrim menus *menú peregrino* are generally available for around €9. If you want to indulge in the wonderful seafood *mariscos* available in Galicia and accompany this with the delightful local *Albariño* wines you can expect to double or treble the basic cost!

Pilgrim hostels *albergues de peregrinos* vary in what they provide but accommodation is usually in bunk beds with additional overflow space on mattresses *colchonetas*. On this route most hostels have been built in recent years and so provide modern facilities. All Xunta (municipal) hostels have a standard charge of €6 and provide a kitchen with basic cooking equipment and a dining / sitting area. Opening times vary depending on the time of year but are generally cleaned and open again from midday to welcome pilgrims. You cannot reserve accommodation in advance and phone numbers are provided for emergency calls only or to check availability outside the normal seasons (most are open all year but can close for holidays or maintenance purposes). Private hostels also offer bunk beds and often additional facilities such as use of washing and drying machines and overnight charges start at €10. Many offer private rooms from around €30.

Galicia: History & Mythology:

What follows is not a scholarly or historical treatise. If you are interested in exploring the subject further you can consult some of the sources listed in the bibliography and carry out your own research. By the same token I make no apology for drawing together some of the innumerable threads that place Finisterre at the heart of the Santiago story, for thus I believe it was. It has remained in obscurity for too long and deserves to be more widely discovered and acknowledged (legends that belong exclusively to Finisterre or Muxía are detailed under their respective headings). But belief and legend should not be confused with the truth to which they point us. As stated in the prologue we may miss the point if we only take the literal view and try and drag the mystical into the factual. The ancient geographers and astronomers like Ptolemy got it wrong; Finisterre is a misnomer for it is not Lands End or the most westerly point in Europe (nor indeed in Spain) but that makes absolutely no difference to its enduring mythology and its power to help shift humankind from a consciousness of fear and separation towards one of unity and love.

• *Megalithic period c. 4000 B.C.*

History tells us little about the Neolithic peoples who inhabited the western fringes of Europe. However, evidence of their stonework can be found all over the Galician landscape and goes back at least 6,000 years as seen in the petroglyphs and rock art of 4,000 B.C. and the dolmens *mamoas* of the same period. These mega-monuments are dotted around Galicia and two fine examples are close to our path; details of these prehistoric temples are provided in the relevant section of this guide. This megalithic culture was deeply religious in nature and left a powerful impact on the peoples who followed.

• *Early Celtic period c. 1000 B.C.*

Central European Celts settled in western Spain inter-marrying with the Iberians. These Celti-Iberians were the forebears of the Celtic Nerios peoples who came to inhabit Galicia centuries before the Roman occupation. Remains of their Celtic villages *castros* can still be seen around the remote countryside. These fortified villages were built in a circular formation usually occupying some elevated ground or hillock. They are found today in place names on maps, but we pass nearby one on Mount Aro during the second stage of this pilgrim route. The extensive mineral deposits of Galicia gave rise to a rich artistic movement and Celtic bronze and gold artefacts from this area can be seen in museums across Europe.

Galicia remains one of the least well known of the Celtic nations and yet it is one of the oldest. Galician Celts trace their mythic lineage to the king of Scythia in the Black sea area where the Druid Caichar had a vision in which he saw them travelling west to found Galicia and Ireland. The first Gaelic colony was established in Galicia under Brath and his son Breogán the latter becoming the legendary hero who founded Brigantium (present day A Coruña) entering folklore and the national anthem of Galicia in the process, *'Wake up from your dreams, home of Breogán.'* His grandson became King Milesius after whom the Celtic Milesians were named. It is generally accepted that the first Celts to settle in Ireland were Milesians from Galicia. In a masterful stroke of genius early Christian monks then extended the Celtic lineage 36 generations back to link it with the biblical Adam.

• *Early Roman period 200 B.C.*

By 200 the Romans controlled most of the southern Iberian peninsular naming the unruly northern province *Hispania Ulterior* to include the area known as *Gallaecia*. In 136 the proconsul Decimus Junius Brutus led his legions across the Lima and Minho rivers to enter Gallaecia for the first time. He met resistance not only from the fierce inhabitants but also from his own soldiers wary of crossing the river *Lima* thought to represent one of the rivers of Hades – the river of forgetfulness *Lethe*. Brutus became the first Roman general to make it to Finisterre and was reputedly mesmerised at the way the sea 'drank up' the sun and was predisposed to the pagan and Druidic worship centred on the Phoenician Altar to the Sun *Ara Solis* The Romans perseverance in conquering this corner of Hispania was, however, more prosaic being primarily due to its rich mining potential.

A Roman garrison was established at Finisterre that would, in time, become the Roman city of Dugium – present day Duio. This early Roman settlement played host to pilgrims from many different traditions and it was to the governor (king) of Dugium that St. James' disciples were directed by queen Lupa for permission to bury his body. Scholars suggest that the busy sea trading port *Artabrorum Portus* mentioned in early historical documents was in fact the port of Dugium with its cross-fertilisation of ideas – just as the Celts and Druids had dovetailed their beliefs into the earlier pagan and Neolithic culture so the Roman's spliced their beliefs onto Celtic lore. The Altar to the Sun *Ara Solis* at Finisterre was a place of both Celtic and Roman veneration. In 61 BC Julius Caesar became governor of Hispania Ulterior and conducted naval expeditions along its shores securing major victories over the Gallaecians. It was during this period that the Romans finally wrested control of the Atlantic seaboard from the Phoenicians.

While the Phoenicians are perhaps best known for their syllabic writing which influenced the Aramaic and Greek alphabets developed from their base at Byblos (from which comes our word Bible) they were the great merchant nation of antiquity becoming undisputed masters of the Mediterranean. They also developed the sea routes to the British Isles to promote the tin trade in particular, helping to develop the Atlantic ports such as Cadiz, Lisbon and Finisterre on the way. They finally came under the control of the Romans in 64 BC. Their cosmogony was largely based around the creative principle as applied to reproduction in nature that in turn depended on fertility and the sun – their *Ara Solis* at Finisterre being the centre of worship of both deities.

• *Early Christian Period c. 40 A.D*

While there is no historical evidence to support the view that St. James preached in Galicia, there are some anecdotal references to that effect. It would appear that he sailed to Galicia, probably Padrón, to preach Christ's message, his body being brought back here after his martyrdom in Jerusalem around 40 A.D. It is reasonable to assume that he, or his followers, would have sought to bring the Christian message specifically to Finisterre. It was common for the early church to seek out places of spiritual significance on which to graft its own message.

Finisterre was one of the most significant spiritual sites in Europe at this time and a major source of Druidic teaching and initiation. It was inevitable that it would draw those with a spiritual mission. It was also directly on the sea route from Palestine to Britannia. Stories abound linking Jesus to both Finisterre and Cornwall which, according to such legends, he visited with his uncle Joseph of Aramathea who earned his wealth from trading with the tin mines there. The *Nine Faces of Christ* portrays Jesus sharing teachings with the Druidic masters during the unaccounted years of his life. If there is substance to these legends then it is conceivable that Jesus may have visited Finisterre before proceeding across the Bay of Biscay to Britain (see mythology). *Artabrorum Portus* was well established at this time and the sea traffic from Palestine to Britannia had no alternative but to pass right by.

• *The Middle Ages 476 – 1453*

Hispania was the Latin name given to the whole Iberian peninsula. After the fall of the Roman Empire in 476 AD the north-western province (present day Galicia) was ruled by the Vandals, the Suevi and the Visigoths. In 711 the Muslim invasion began and its forces quickly moved north to conquer the whole peninsular, capturing the bells of Santiago cathedral along the way and infamously taking them to Granada. But Galicia proved impossible to control and Islamic rule here lasted only a few decades. It was to take another 700 years before the re-conquest was complete in the south – and the bells returned to Santiago.

• *The Catholic Monarchs 1469 – 1516*

The marriage in 1469 of Isabella I of Castille and Fernando II of Aragón saw the merging of 2 of the most powerful kingdoms in Spain. The title Catholic Monarchs *los Reyes Católicos* was bestowed by Pope Alexander VI with an eye to aiding the re-conquest and unifying Spain under Roman Catholicism. This was finally achieved after the conquest of the Muslim Kingdom of Granada in 1492, the same year Columbus 'discovered' the Americas. This illustrious period was tarnished by the expulsion or massacre of non-Catholics under the infamous Inquisition initiated under her reign. Isabella is, perhaps, best remembered for her more beneficent activities such as the building of the pilgrim hospital in Santiago, now the luxurious Hostal of the Catholic Monarchs *parador Hostal Dos Reis Católicos* – reputedly the oldest hotel in the world in continuous occupation for that purpose.

• War of Independence and Carlist Wars 1808 – 1873

Despite its remote location, Galicia was not spared the effects of the War of Independence 'Peninsular War.' Forces of Napoleon ransacked many of the villages along which you will pass including both Finisterre and Muxía themselves. It was during the Carlist Wars 1833 – 1876 that the intrepid missionary George Borrow arrived in Spain to spread the New Testament. His eventful journeys are documented in *The Bible in Spain* first published in 1842. He set out to preach the Gospel to the 'peasants' of Finisterre and was promptly arrested by the local inhabitants as none other than King Don Carlos himself, eventually convincing the mayor of Corcubión that he was merely a humble missionary. Borrow makes a fascinating read and his sketch of Galicia, her culture and legends has recently been reprinted (see Bibliography).

• First Spanish Republic and The Franco Period 1873 – 1975

Towards the end of the 3rd Carlist war the first Spanish Republic was proclaimed in 1873. Again the remoteness of Galicia was no bar to its involvement in anti-monarchist activities. Indeed its resistance to any outside interference continues to this day. In 1936 General Franco seized power leading to one of the bloodiest civil wars in history. That same year the Gelegust party led by Castelao first presented the idea of an independent Galician State *Estatuto de Galicia* to the Spanish Parliament. Despite various initiatives to earn independence for Galicia it was not until 1981 that it achieved a measure of autonomy, being recognised as a separate autonomous region in that year.

• Galicia Today 1975 –

After Franco's death in 1975, King Carlos nominally succeeded and appointed political reformist Adolfo Suárez to form a government. In 1982 the socialist party (PSOE) won a sweeping victory under Felipe González who successfully steered Spain into full membership of the EEC in 1986. In 1996 José María Aznar, leader of the right wing *Partido Popular* (PP), won a narrow mandate but in November 2002 the oil tanker Prestige ran into a storm off Finisterre and the ensuing ecological catastrophe sank not only the livelihood of scores of Galician fisherman but, in due time, the right wing government as well resulting in a popular cry up and down the country of 'never again' *nunca maís*. It only took the government's unpopular support of the invasion of Iraq coupled with the Madrid bombings in March 2004 to put the socialist's back in power under the youthful leadership of José Luis Rodríguez Zapatero. The new government set in motion an immediate change in foreign policy and, more controversially, a sudden but decisive shift from a conservative Catholic to a liberal secular society that led to one newspaper headline, 'Church and State square up in struggle for the spirit of Spain.' The deepening economic and Euro crisis led to the election of Mariano Rajoy of the centre-right PP in December 2011... and seemingly immune to all these social and political upheavals, the *Camino Finisterre* goes quietly about her gentle spirit of transformation.

Galician Culture: The flowering of Galician art that took place under Alfonso VII and Ferdinand II (kings of Galicia until it was absorbed into León and Castille under Ferdinand III) saw the completion of the great cathedrals of Ourense, Lugo and Tui, as well as Santiago. However, between the three great powers comprising the Catholic monarchy, the Aristocracy and Castille; Galician art, culture and language were greatly diluted. Indeed while the French Way *Camino Francés* introduced wonderfully inspiring European art and artisans to towns all along the route to Santiago, it had the effect of diminishing the Celtic influences within Galicia.

Galician Language: The distinctive language of Galicia *Gallego* is still widely used today. The language institute estimates that 94% of the population understand it, while 88% can speak it. Galego belongs to the Iberian Romance group of languages with some common aspects with Portuguese. Phrase books between Spanish *Castellano* Galician *Galego* and English are difficult to find but one of the more obvious differences is the substitution of the Spanish J – hard as in Junta (pron: **kh**unta) as opposed to the softer Galego Xunta (pron: **sh**unta). Here are a few common phrases to help distinguish one from the other.

The Jacobean Way	Del Camino Jacobeo	Do Camiño Xacobeo
Pilgrimage to Finisterre	Peregrinaje a Finisterre	Peregrinaxe a Fisterra
Fountains of Galicia	Las Fuentes de Galicia	Das Fontes de Galiza
The Botanical garden	El Jardin Botanico	O Xardín Botánico
Museum of sacred art	Un Museo de Arte Sacro	O Museu do Arte Sacro
Collegiate church	Colegiata Iglesia	Colexiata Igrexa
Town Hall	Casa Consistorial	Concello da Vila
Below the main Square	Bajo el plaza mayor	Debaixo do praza maior

The Revival *Rexurdimento* of Galician language and literature in the 19th century was spearheaded with the publication in 1863 of *Cantares Gallegos* by the incomparable Galician poetess, Rosalía Castro. The Revival reached its zenith in the 1880's with the publication of many illuminating Galician texts such as *Follas Novas* also by Rosalía Castro, *Saudades Galegas* by Lamas de Carvajal and *Queixumes dos Pinos* by Eduardo Pondal. Galicia's culture has been kept alive as much by its exiles, political and economic, as by those that remained behind. The unofficial anthem of Galicia, The Pines *Os Pinos* was written and first sung in South America where it urged the Galician people to awaken from the yoke of servitude into freedom: *'Listen to the voices of the murmuring pines which is none other than the voices of the Galician people.'* However, even the pine trees seem under threat from the imported eucalyptus that has taken over large swathes of the countryside.

The fruits of this revival can be tasted, nonetheless, throughout Galicia today. You may well hear the swirl of the traditional Galician bagpipes *Gaita* in the bars of Santiago or Finisterre or at one of its many festivals and fairs that take place throughout the year. Many of these are based on the ancient Celtic celebration of the seasons particularly at the equinoxes and the summer and winter solstices. The short pilgrimages to local shrines *romerías* endorse the deeply held religious values of the people of Galicia but drawing ever larger crowds are the secular festivals such as the gastronomic feast and discotheque *Festa do Longueiron* in Finisterre, now in its 25th year.

Galician Nationalism appears to be born more out of a deep pride in its traditions, rather than a need to overthrow a culture that has been imposed from outside. This is not unlike other Celtic cultures that have found themselves marginalised on the Western fringes of Europe. We demean Galicia and ourselves by stereotyping popular Spanish culture onto her. This is not the Spain of castanets, paella and Rioja wines. Her identity is clearly Celtic with gaitas, mariscos and Albariño wines predominating – all of which are a cause of justified pride.

The past suffering of Galicia is perhaps best summed up in the compelling poems of **Rosalía de Castro**. The following extract provides a flavour of her unrivalled prowess as the humble spokesperson for the people of Galicia and their unique culture. Her work has been beautifully edited and translated by Anna-Marie Aldaz, Barbara N. Gantt, and Anne C. Bromley (see bibliography). In the following prologue to *New Leaves* we can sense the inner alchemy of her life transforming her fight against oppression into the purest gold of forgiveness – the purpose, perhaps, of all true pilgrims.

> *Here then are the follas novas that should actually be called 'old' since that is what they are. They are also 'last' because now that I have paid the debt I felt I owed my country, it is unlikely that I will write more poems in our native tongue. They go forth, not in search of triumph, but of forgiveness; not of praise, but of forgetting; not of the acclaim of previous times, but of the goodwill given to bad books. 'Let them pass!' This is what I wish: that you let them pass by like another sound, like a rustic fragrance – a fragrance which brings up something of that poetry that is born in the vast solitude, in the evergreen fields of our land, and along our beautiful seashores. Such poetry comes directly to us, looking for a natural refuge in our hearts that suffer and care for our beloved land of Galicia.*

This simple guidebook has been researched and written by a fellow pilgrim and I trust it will serve to make the journey ahead more meaningful for you. As you set off into the heart of Galicia I offer you this ancient Celtic prayer to bless the journey ahead.

> *May the road rise to meet you*
> *May the wind be always at your back*
> *May the sun shine full upon your face*
> *May the rain fall soft upon your fields, and*
> *Until we meet again*
> *May God hold you*
> *In the hollow of Her hand.*

The journey begins...

Arriving Sarria: The majority of pilgrims arrive in Sarria by bus from Santiago via Lugo; approx. hourly throughout the week from the main bus station in Santiago with [1] Alsa (www.alsa.es) via La Coruña 2½ hours €12. [2] Freire (www.empresafreire. com) this bus also stops at Santiago airport (SCQ) Aeropuerto de Labacolla. Lugo to Sarria with Monbus approx. hourly throughout the day with journey time ½ hour €2. / Monbus (www.monbus.es) provide a direct service from Santiago to Sarria daily departing 18:00 arriving Sarria at 20:45 €8. Rail with average journey time 4 hours (via Orense).

Pilgrim Facilities: Pilgrim passport *credencial* available at the Pilgrim office in Santiago or Iglesia de Santa Mariña on rúa Maior in Sarria. Pilgrims with physical or other problems can arrange for **backpack transfers** *transporte de mochilas* between reserved private accommodation (it is not possible to reserve in Xunta hostels). Contact Xacotrans: http://www.xacotrans.com/ or phone: +34 982 639 300. For l**uggage storage** in Santiago you can send items to Ivar Rekve for collection: https://www.caminodesantiago.me/luggage-storage-in-santiago-de-compostela/ phone: (+34) 603 466 490.

Arriving / Departing Santiago: Travel costs vary widely but several budget airlines now compete for the traffic into Santiago international airport at Lavacolla. *Empresa Freire* offers a regular bus service from/to Lavacolla to the city centre.
•**Air:** *Easyjet* flies from London Gatwick and Geneva. *Ryanair* from London Stansted, Frankfurt, Rome, Madrid, Malaga, Barcelona, Alicante. *Vueling* fly from Paris. *Air Berlin* fly from major destinations throughout Europe to Santiago via their hub in La Palma Majorca. *Aer Lingus* fly Santiago direct from Dublin (summer schedule) and *BA / Iberia* and other major airlines offer regular services throughout the year via various connecting airports in Spain, mainly Madrid. Check other possibilities from / to nearby airports at La Corunna, Vigo and Porto – all of which have regular rail and bus connections to/from Santiago.
•**Rail:**   you can book online through Spanish rail network RENFE *www.renfe.es/ horarios/english* or Rail Europe at *www.raileurope.co.uk.*
•**Bus:** you can book online (paypal only) with Alsa *www.alsa.es* (English language option + St. James Way page for route options).
•**Ferry:** The advantage of sailing is that you get a chance to acclimatise slowly – check with Brittany Ferries (Santander - Portsmouth) and P&O (Bilbao - Plymouth).
•**Car Hire:** a relatively cheap (esp. if sharing the cost) and convenient way to travel on to such places as Santander or Bilbao and flying or sailing home from there. This option is only practicable within Spain as drop-off in another country (i.e Portugal or France) is prohibitively expensive.

TRAVEL NOTES:

_____
_____
_____
_____
_____
_____
_____
_____
_____
_____

SARRIA: with its Celtic origins was a major medieval centre for pilgrims with churches, chapels, monasteries and no less than 7 pilgrim hospitals. The ancient atmosphere can still be felt in the attractive old quarter that climbs the old granite steps *Escalinata Maior* to the central hub of pilgrim Sarria *rúa Maior*.

Historical monuments: These are conveniently located along *rúa Maior* passing: ❶ *Iglesia de Santa Mariña XIX* with its evocative pilgrim mural (*credenciales* issued after pilgrim mass daily at 18:00 / Sun 12:00). At the top of rúa Maior ❷ *Iglesia del Salvador XIII* with its tympanum of Christ in Majesty and the Tree of Life (mass Sun 18:00). ❸ *Hospital de San Anton XVI* original pilgrim hostel now the Courts of Justice. ❹ *Fortaleza de Sarria y Torres XIII* castle (ruins). ❺ *Mosteiro de Santa María Madalena (Convento de la Merced) XIII* with fine plateresque façade and now an albergue which also issues *credenciales.* Daily mass at 18:30 / Sun 13:00. *(Note all indicated times are liable to last minute changes so check beforehand).* The camino continues down to the medieval bridge *Ponte Áspera (Rough Bridge)* over the río Celerio.

Sarria is a bustling modern town with a population of 13,500. It has become a major starting point for pilgrims with limited time but providing the minimum distance required (100 km by foot) entitling the pilgrim to apply for a *compostela* at Santiago, hence the profusion of pilgrim hostels in town providing lodging for budding pilgrims arriving by bus and rail. The advent of the railway in the 19th century saw the town develop eastwards leaving the ancient *camino real* largely intact.

New arrivals are joined by seasoned pilgrims, many arriving by foot from France and the route becomes very busy from this point onwards. If you are just starting out on your pilgrimage note that a few hardened 'veterans' can sometimes begrudge the sudden appearance of new pilgrims on 'their' camino but a smile melts even the most hardened heart and you will generally find welcome and assistance wherever you look for it.

Pilgrim services abound in Sarria: ❏ *Turismo Vigo de Sarria* Ⓒ 982 530 099. ❏ *Peregrinoteca* Ⓒ +34 982 530 190 calle Benigno Quiroga, 16 - Bajo / *Escalinata Maior* a veritable Aladdin's Cave of equipment exclusive to pilgrims with the ever helpful wizard *José Mª Díaz Bernárdez* (see photo below) to equip you with all those items you forgot to pack... from ponchos to plasters.

Accommodation: (see town plan) on the outskirts of Sarria in *Vigo de Sarria:* **Camping Vila de Sarria** *[12÷1]*+ ©️ 982 535 467 €6+ & opp: *P** **Ana** ©️ 982 531 458 €24+. *Alb.*● **A Pedra** *Priv.*[14÷3]*+ €10 ©️ 982 530 130 adj. *Turismo* & opp: *Alb.*● **Oasis** *Priv.[27÷4]* €10 ©️ 605 948

644. *Sarria 'new town'* on busy *Calvo Sotelo* @N° 198 *Hs* **dpCristal** ©️ 669 799 512 €30 also @N° 199 *Alb.*● **Alma do Camiño** *Priv.[96÷10]* €6–9 ©️ 982 876 768 m: 629 822 036. Along *Rúa do Peregrino* @N° 50 *Alb.*● **Credencial** *Priv.[96÷10]* €6–9 ©️ 982 876 455 m: 639 722 878 also @N° 23 *Alb.*● **Puente Ribeira** *Priv.[40÷4]* €7–10 ©️ 982 876 789 m: 698 175 619 adj. *H***** **Alfonso IX** €55+ ©️ 982 530 005. Popular *H*** **Oca Villa** €45 ©️ 982 533 873 (left 100m) Benigno Quiroga 4-9.

Sarria *'old town' [km. 111,5] on rúa Maior:* **Albergues ❶ – ❾** (Av. price €10). @N°75 ❶ **Casa Peltre** *Priv* *[22÷3]* ©️ 606 226 067. @N°76 *P****Escalinata** ©️ 982 530 259. @N°64 ❷ **Mayor** *Priv.[16÷2]* ©️ 646 427 734. Down (right) @N°79 ❸ **Xunta** *[40÷2]* ©️ 660 396 813 (€6). S/o up @N°62 *Hs****Oneseason** *O Abrigadoiro* ©️ 616 989 703. @N°44 ❹ **O Durmiñento** *Priv.[40÷7]*+ ©️ 982 531 099. @N°57 ❺ **Internacional** *Priv.[44÷4]*+ ©️ 982 535 109 café + roof-top terrace. @N°49 ❻ **O Obradoiro** *Priv.[28÷2]* ©️ 982 532 442. @N°31 ❼ **Los Blasones** *Priv.*[42÷4]* ©️ 600 512 565 + rear patio. @N°19 *P** **Mesón Camino Francés** ©️ 982 532 351 (opp. Mesón O Tapas). *Concello / Plaza de la Constitución* and @N°10 ❽ **Don Álvaro** *Priv.[40÷4]* ©️ 982 531 592 with rear patio. @N°4 (entrance off Conde de Lemos, 10) ❾ **Matías** *Priv.[30÷2]*+ ©️ 982 534 285 (part of restaurant Matias Locanda Italiana). ● Additional albergues: ● **Dos Oito Marabedís** *Priv.[24÷7]* ©️ 629 461 770 rúa Conde de Lemos, 23 modern terraced house. 300m further up ● **Barbacoa** *Priv.[10÷1]*+ ©️ 619 879 476 c/Esqueirodos,1. On the *far* side of rua Maior; 400m down rua da Calexa ● **San Lázaro** *Priv.[30÷4]*+ ©️ 982 530 626 c/San Lázaro,7 and at the top of town (out of the bustle) ● **Monasterio la Magdalena** *Priv.[90÷3]* Av. de la Merced, ©️ 982 533 568 'twinned' with albergue Seminario Menor in Santiago. ❏ **Other accommodation:** *P* **Matias Rooms** €25-40 Calle Rosalia de Castro, 19 (same ownership as Albergue Matias ©️ 982 534 285). In the 'new' town *P** **Casa Matías** €25 ©️ 659 160 498 Calvo Sotelo,39 and to the rear in rúa Formigueiros *H** **Mar de Plata** ©️ 982 530 724. Adj. railway station *Hr** **Roma** ©️ 982 532 211 Calvo Sotelo,2. ❏ Variety of lively cafes around the rúa Maior. For a tranquil setting on the river try *O Chanto* perched on the río Sarria with access via delightful river path.

rio Celeiro

Ponte Áspera

Camiño Francés

SALIDA

San Roque
Cementerio

5 **Monasterio de la Magdalena**

A **Monasterio de la Magdalena**
·credencial

A **San Lázaro**

Estación Ferrocarril

rúa José Antonio

Roma H

Parque Do Bosque

Campo da Feira

rúa da Mercede

rúa Calexa

rúa Porvir

Fortaleza de Sarria
(Ruinas)

Torre **4**

rúa do Castelo

Cruceiro

A **Barbacoa**

Sarmiento

rúa Nova

Casa Matías

P

Mar de Plata H

El Salvador **2**

3 **San Anton**

Matias Locanda Italiana

Dos Oito A **Don Álvaro**
Marabedís

Matías **9** **8**

Plaza

P Camiño Francés

Concello

7 **Los Blasones**
6 **Obradoiro**
5 **Internacional**
1 **Santa Mariña**
·credencial

rúa Calvo Sotelo

O'Durmiñento **4**

OneSeason O Abrigadoiro P
Mayor **2**

r/Maior

3 **Xunta**

rúa Matías López

Estación de Autobuses
(Santiago via Lugo)

Casa Peltre **1**
Escalinata Maior →

P **Escalinata**

rúa Benigno Quiroga

Oca Villa H

Ferreiro

■ *Peregrinoteca (equipamiento)*
© 982-530 190

rúa Diego Pazos

SARRIA
(Pop. 13,500 – Alt. 455m)

Parque O Chanto

rio Sarria

Malecón

A **Puente Ribeira**

H **Alfonso IX***

rúa do Peregrino

Campo do río

rúa Calvo Sotelo

rio Sarria

Credencial A

A **Alma do Camiño**

VIGO DE SARRIA

Cristal P

Turismo © 982-530 099

O

Puesta del Sol

S ——— N

Oasis A

i A **A Pedra**

ENTRADA

Salida del Sol

E

❐ **To err is human, to forgive, divine.**

———————————————— *Alexander Pope*

01 115.1 km (71.5 ml) – Santiago

SARRIA – PORTOMARÍN

‖‖‖‖‖‖‖‖‖	12.1 --- ---	55%
▬▬▬	10.0 --- ---	45%
▬▬	0.0	
Total km	**22.1 km** (13.7 ml)	

◣ 23.6 km (+1.5 km)

Alto ▲ Momientos 660m (2,165 ft)

< Ⓐ Ⓗ > Barbadelo ❶ **3.6** – ❺ **4.5** km – Morgade **12.1** km – Ferreiros **13.5** km – Mercadoiro **16.9** km.

❐ **The Practical Path:** The majority of today's stage is on lovely woodland paths and gravel tracks *sendas*. Apart from the bare flanks around the high point on the Peña do Cervo at Momientos (above Portomarín) much of the remainder is along tree-lined roads. So we have good shade from the sun or shelter from the driving rain. We will pass through many small hamlets that seem to blend seamlessly one into the next. Several new cafés offer refreshment stops along the way.

❐ **The Mystical Path:** Two ancient Orders occupied opposite sides of this river but their strongholds are long gone now buried under the flood waters created by the dam to serve the insatiable demands of a new generation. We cannot live in the past and we try in vain to live with the idea of some future golden age. The only place we can truly inhabit is the present. The rest is fantasy – some painful, some pleasurable – both deceptive.

❐ **Personal Reflections:** *"… I reflect on the extraordinary revelation of the third secret of Fátima. We are all fallen angels struggling to find our wings so that we can fly back home to the Divine. If God is my Father what does that make me and, by extension, all my fellow brothers and sisters? We each share the same Identity and the same Inheritance. And so I come full circle, back to the place where I began and to the realisation that the only way out... is in. The only way off the mortal coil is through the total forgiveness of self, other and the world. That is why external authority must collapse. The Voice for God is within and urges each one of us, as children of one God, to become the authors of own awakening …"*

0.0 km **Sarria** *Centro* from albergue ❶ in Sarria (or from wherever you stayed the night) head up c/Mayor past the church of Santa Mariña with its sombre medieval pilgrim murals and past the town hall (left) *Casa do Concello*. Next we pass the

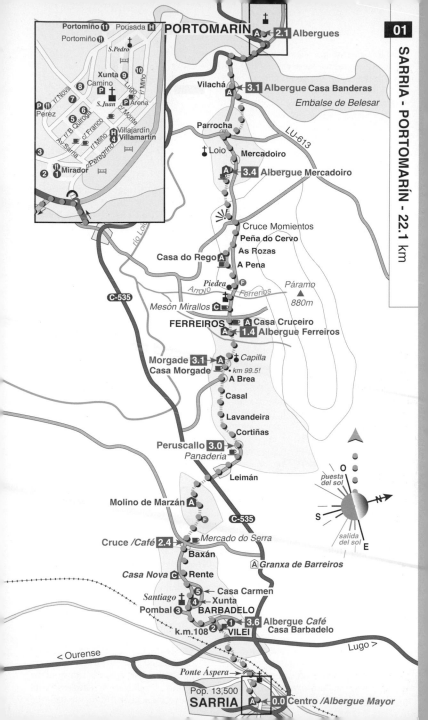

PORTOMARÍN Ⓐ ▸ **2.1** ▸ **Albergues**

Vilachá Ⓐ ▸ **3.1** ▸ Albergue Casa Banderas

Embalse de Belesar

LU-613

Parrocha

†Loio

Mercadoiro

Ⓐ ▸ **3.4** ▸ Albergue Mercadoiro

Cruce Momientos

Peña do Cervo

As Rozas

Casa do Rego Ⓐ

A Pena

Piedra † Ⓕ *Ferreiros*

Arroyo *Páramo*

Mesón Mirallos Ⓒ ▲ *880m*

FERREIROS Ⓐ Casa Cruceiro

Ⓐ ▸ **1.4** ▸ Albergue Ferreiros

Morgade **3.1** Ⓐ † *Capilla*

Casa Morgade ▸ *km 99.5!*

A Brea

Casal

Lavandeira

Cortiñas

Peruscallo **3.0** ▸

Panaderia

Leimán

Molino de Marzán Ⓐ

Ⓕ

C-535

Cruce /*Café* **2.4** ▸ *Mercado do Serra*

Baxán

Ⓐ *Granxa de Barreiros*

Casa Nova Ⓒ Rente

← Casa Carmen

Santiago † ④ ← Xunta

Pombal ③ **BARBADELO**

k.m.108 ② ① ▸ **3.6** ▸ Albergue *Café*

VILEI Casa Barbadelo

< Ourense Lugo >

Ponte Áspera →

Pop. 13,500 Ⓐ ▸ **0.0** ▸ Centro /Albergue Mayor

SARRIA

Inset map (Portomarín)

Portomiño ⑪ Pousada Ⓗ

Portomiño ⑪

†S.Pedro

Xunta ⑨ ⑩

Camino †

⑧ P S.Juan P Ⓒ r/Nova

Pérez P ⑪ ⑥ r/B.Quiroga c/Franco

⑤ Villajardin Ⓗ Villamartín

③ r/Monte ④

② ① r/Peregrino

Mirador

Río Loio

intimate *Praza da Constitución* with its albergues, cafes and restaurants and towards the top of the street (left) Church of St. Saviour *Igrexa de San Salvador XIII^{th}C* with its primitive Romanesque tympanum over the main door. Opposite was St. Anthony's pilgrim Hospice *Hospital de San Anton* (now courts of Justice) and here we turn right> to pass the ruins of the Sarria castle *Fortaleza de*

Sarria (left) only one of the 4 original towers remains. [The castle was destroyed during the uprising of the peasantry against the aristocracy in the 15th century known as the *Irmandiños].* We pass a stone *cruceiro* (right) with fine views back over the town and up past the country market *Campo da Feira* (left) which has existed here since the 14th century and down to the plasteresque façade of the **Mosteiro da Madalena [0.7** km] originally instituted in the 13th century, later coming under the Augustinian rule. We finally head down past the cemetery and *Capela de San Lázaro* to cross the road and río Celeiro over the medieval **Ponte Áspera [0.5** km] 'Rough Bridge' which describes its coarsely cut stone. A path now winds between river and rail before crossing the line in *Santi Michaelis* thence under road viaduct across a stream to climb up through delightful ancient woodland to join the road in **Vilei** an extension of **Barbadelo [2.4** km].

3.6 km Barbadelo *Vilei Alb.* ❶ Casa **Barbadelo** *Priv.[68÷12]+* €9-12 ℂ 982 531 934 with garden and swimpool. ❷ **108 km** *Priv.[12÷5]+* €8-29 ℂ 634 894 524. ❸ O Pombal *Priv.[12÷1]* €9 ℂ 686 718 732. 200m off route below *Igrexa de Santiago XII^{th}C* Romanesque with a fine tympanum and statue of St. James. Pilgrim mass at 19:00 (check notice board). *[The area is known locally as Mosteiro in reference to a monastery founded here as*

early as the 9th century]. ❹ **Barbadelo** *Xunta.[18÷2]* €6 ℂ former school house on **village green [0.7** km]. Behind the albergue is a summer cantina and at the top of the lane (200m off route) ❺ **Casa de Carmen** *Priv.[26÷3]+* €9-35 ℂ 982 532 294 in restored 17^{th}c farmhouse with terrace and private chapel *Capela de San Silvestre.* Continue to **Rente [1.0** km] *CR* Casa Nova ℂ 982 187 854 s/o along woodland paths through ancient oak and chestnut groves and cross main road **[0.7** km]:

2.4 km Cruce *Café Mercado do Serra (right + 1.8 km Alb.* **Granxa de Barreiros** *Priv.[46÷8]+* €10 +18 ℂ 982 533 656 *Ortoá LU-633).* S/o past *[F.]* to *Alb.* **Molino de Marzán** *Priv.[16÷1]* €10 ℂ 679 438 077. Cross road into **Leimán** and **Peruscallo.**

2.9 km Peruscallo *Panaderia Peruscallo.* S/o through **Corntiñas, Lavandeira, Casal** and into **A Brea [2.1** km] passing (km 99,5) into **Morgade [1.0** km]:

3.1 km Morgade *Alb.* **Casa Morgade** *Priv.[6÷1]+* €10-28 ℂ 982 531 250 with popular café (if busy continue to Ferreiros). Pass stone chapel and continue on track down (through!) the Ferreiros stream. This is rural Galicia at her best; green and often wet underfoot with the earthy smell of cow dung. Narrow laneways with granite stepping-stones raised above flood levels provide a gentle climb up to:

1.4 km **Ferreiros** *Mesón Casa Cruceiro*
the traditional edifice overlooked by its
ultra modern *Alb.* ❶ **Casa Cruceiro** *Priv.*
[12÷1]+ €10-40 ℂ 982 541 240. Just
below the café (left) ❷ **Ferreiros** *Xunta.*
[22÷1] €6 ℂ 660 396 815 (Primitiva)
former schoolhouse set in leafy glade.
[Ferreiros translates as blacksmith]. S/o
past **Mirallos [0.3** km] *Mesón Mirallos*

café (+ colchones €-donativo) adj. the Church of Santa María and just beyond the
ancient ❖ *Chalice Stone* up to the tranquil hamlet of **A Pena [0.4** km] *Alb.* ♥ **Casa
do Rego** *Priv.[6÷1]+* €10 ℂ 982 167 812 with a warm welcome in 7 languages!
Café *menú* and outdoor terrace. Up steeply to **As Rozas [0.8** km] *[F.]* and the high
point *Pena dos Corvos 660m* at Cruce Momientos **[1.3** km] with fine views over the
reservoir as we begin our descent into the río Miño valley and **Mercadoiro [0.7** km]:

3.4 km **Mercadoiro** *Alb.* **Mercadoiro**
& café Bodeguiña Priv.[32÷6]+ €10-40 ℂ
982 545 359. Popular café-restaurant with
pilgrim menu in delightful hamlet with
an official population of – one! Continue
through **Moutras** and **A Parrocha.** *[off
route left is the remote valley of Loio
with the ruins of the Monastery of Santa
María de Loio – birthplace of the Order
of Santiago in the 12th century].* The route

crosses several country lanes to drop down steeply on rough asphalt lane into:

3.1 km **Vilachá** *Alb.* **Casa Banderas** *Priv.[8÷1]+* €10-40 ℂ 982 545 391 the
South African flag pointing to the owner's nationality. Snacks available from adj.
Casa Susanna (donations provide sustenance for tomorrow's pilgrims). Now we
follow the road and make our way over the bridge spanning the deep Miño basin to
the **roundabout [2.0** km] at Portomarín. *[To continue to Gonzar follow the road to
the left over the second bridge (200m) see next stage].* Or take the steep staircase
in front, part of the original medieval bridge across the river Miño. These lead up
to the arch and *capela de Santa María de las Nieves* which, along with several
other historic monuments, were all removed to the high ground around Portomarín
when the dam was built across the river to create the Belesar reservoir in 1962. *[The
original bridge was of Roman origin and joined the district of San Pedro, with links
to the Knights of Santiago, with San Nicolás (headquarters of the Knights of Saint
John). The river formed a major strategic boundary].* Climb the stairs for the lower
2 **albergues [0.2** km] with fine views over the river and reservoir.

2.2 km **Portomarín** *Albergue. Alb.* ❶
O Mirador *Priv.[27÷6]* €10 ℂ 982 545
323 first hostel as we enter town with
mirador bar/restaurant above fine view
over rio Miño. Adj. ❷ **Ferramenteiro**
Priv.*[130÷1] €10 ℂ 982 545 362
purpose-built hostel. ❸ **Folgueira** *Priv.*
[32÷1] €10 ℂ 982 545 166 Av. Chantada
(on way out) The centre and main action
is at the top end of town ½ km further on.

Continue up the cobbled main street *rúa Xeral Franco* with its handsome stone colonnades with various shops and cafés leading to the central square *Praza Conde de Fenosa* and its choice of restaurants, bars and pensiónes and the hub of the town's action. Here we also find the *Casa do Concello* and *Correos* and overlooking all this activity is the austere Romanesque fortress church of St. John due to its links with the Knights of Saint John. *Igrexa de San Juan / San Xoán* (also Saint Nicholas). It was painstakingly rebuilt from its original site now submerged under the waters of the Balesar reservoir and ascribed to the workshop of Master Mateo

who carved the Portico de Gloria in Santiago. Built as both a place of worship and defence, with its 4 defensive towers and battlements (crenellated parapet). The church has a single barrel vaulted nave and semicircular apse and prominent rose window *(see photo right)*. Daily mass at 20:00 (Sundays 12:30). Times may vary.

Pilgrim hostels: See town plan for location: *Albergue* ❹ **Villamartín** *Priv. [20÷2]* €10 ✆ 982 545 054 part of the popular hotel Villajardín on rúa de Miño and overlooking the park and river to the rear. ❺ **Novo Porto** *Priv.[22÷1]* €10 ✆ 982 545 277 excellent modern facilities on c/Benigno Quiroga 12. Adj. at Nº6 ❻ **El Caminante** *Priv.[12÷1]+* €10 ✆ 982 545 176 (+15 priv. rooms €40). Nearby on c/Diputación Nº9 ❼ **Ultreia** *Priv.[14÷1]+* €10 ✆ 982 545 067 opp. at Nº8 ❽ **Porto Santiago** *Priv.*[14÷1]+* ✆ 618 826 515 & small terrace off side entrance. ❾ **Portomarín** *Xunta.[110÷6]* €6 ✆ 982 545 143. The original hostel recently renovated with all modern facilities and washing and drying machines at rear. ●10 **Manuel** *Priv.[16÷1]+* €10-25 ✆ 982 545 385 & adj. pension. ●11 **Portomiño** *Priv. [10÷1]+* ✆ 982 547 575 reception at restaurant/bar on corner of Av. Sarria.

Other accommodation: *in addition to the private pensión rooms offered in the albergues marked +*: In the central square (with lively restaurants) *P°* **Posada del Camino** ✆ 982 545 081. *P°°***Arenas** ✆ 982 545 386. Nearby in rúa de Miño,14 *H°°* **Villajardín** ✆ 982 545 054 and at the top end of town and price bracket: *H°°°* **Pousada de Portomarín** ✆ 982 545 200 adj. to Parque Antonio Sanz and nearby Church of Saint Peter *Iglesia San Pedro* with fine Romanesque doorway. *[Next albergue: Gonzar – 8.2 km].*

REFLECTIONS:

*"My journey of awakening has truly begun and continues according to my intentions.
I will endeavour to make every step a prayer for peace and wholeness... holiness."*

K.90
RIO MIÑO
Embalse de Belesar

❏ **The foolish man seeks happiness in the distance;**
The wise man grows it under his feet.
—————————————— *J R Oppenheimer*

02 **93.0** km (57.8 ml) – Santiago

PORTOMARÍN – PALAS DE REI

⋯⋯⋯⋯⋯	--- ---	19.9	--- ---	80%
▬▬▬▬	--- ---	4.9	--- ---	20%
▬▬▬▬	--- ---	0.0		
Total km		**24.8 km** (15.4 ml)		

▲▲▲	--- ---	27.0 km (^450m +2.2 km)
Alto ▲	Sierra Ligonde 720m (2,362 ft)	

< Ⓐ Ⓗ > Gonzar **7.8** km – Hospital **11.5** – Ventas de Narón **12.9** km –Ligonde **16.6** km – Eirexe **17.2** km – Portos **19.3** km – Os Chacotes **23.6** km.

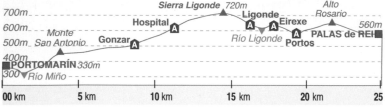

❏ **The Practical Path:** A day of varied terrain as we start by climbing up through woodland around the *Embalse de Belesar* to join the main road which we have to cross on several occasions before leaving it to climb the *Sierra Ligonde* descending to Portos which offers us the detour to Vilar de Donas. Then comes a gentler climb around the side of Rosary Heights *Alto Rosario* to drop down finally to Palas de Rei. Prepare for an early start if you intend to take the detour to Vilas de Donas.

❏ **The Mystical Path:** Will you make time to detour to this mystical resting place of the Knights of Saint James? Here effigies of the knights in their armour are watched over by the beautiful frescoes that adorn the walls of this sacred temple dedicated to Saint Saviour. A pilgrim must travel on two paths simultaneously. The tourist will look for the stone altar – the pilgrim an altered state. The one seeks sacred sites – the other in-sight. Will you make time today to detour into the inner mystery?

❏ **Personal Reflections:** "... *The incessant rain pounds down as heavy as when it started a week ago. The country is awash; roads have turned to rivers; rivers to torrents. I sat for a while at the base of the ancient oak and felt its solid support and in the same instant knew that my period of silence was ended. I don't know how long I been in this altered state, induced as much by physical exhaustion as any ecstatic revelation. And I don't know how long they had been there but they helped me to my feet and we embraced in love and respect for the experiences we had each invoked; 3 pilgrims from 3 different countries with 3 different languages but part of one family. I found it hard to speak after such a long spell of silence but I managed to say 'bless you' realising that with every breath I send out positive or negative vibrations. Regardless of outer conditions I can choose to send out love. Until that moment I had not noticed the ancient wayside cross silently witnessing this loving reunion of fellow pilgrims ...*"

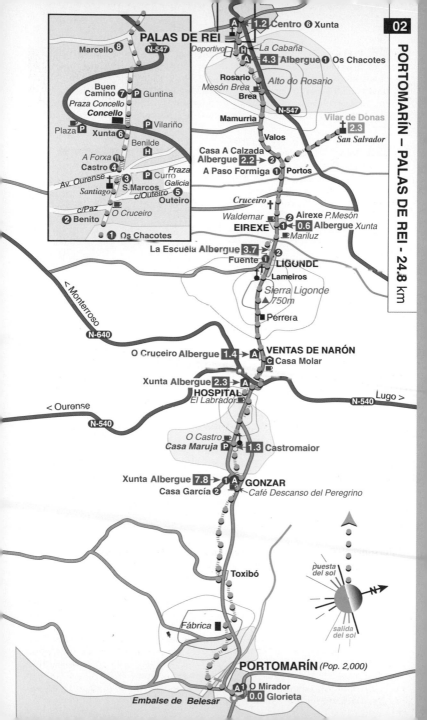

PALAS DE REI

Marcello **8**   N-547

A **1.2** Centro **6** Xunta

Deportivo   H   *La Cabaña*

A **4.3** Albergue **1** Os Chacotes

Rosario   *Alto do Rosario*

Mesón Brea   **Brea**

Buen Camino **7**   P Guntina

Praza Concello   **Concello**

P Vilariño

Plaza P   Xunta **6**

Benilde   H

Mamurria   N-547

Valos   Vilar de Donas †

2.3

San Salvador

A Forxa **1**

Castro **4**   *Praza*   P Curro   *Galicia*

Av. Ourense †   **3**   S.Marcos   c/Outeiro   **5**

Santiago   **Outeiro**

c/Paz   *O Cruceiro*

2 *Benito*

1 Os Chacotes

Casa A Calzada

Albergue **2.2** → **2**

A Paso Formiga **1**   Portos

Cruceiro †

Waldemar   Airexe P.Mesón

1 → **2**   **0.6** Albergue *Xunta*

EIREXE   *Mariluz*

La Escuela Albergue **3.7** → **2**

Fuente **1**   **LIGONDE**

Lameiros

Sierra Ligonde

▲ *750m*

Perrera

O Cruceiro Albergue **1.4** → A   **VENTAS DE NARÓN**

C Casa Molar

Xunta Albergue **2.3** → A

HOSPITAL   *El Labrador*

< Monterroso   N-640

< Ourense   N-540   Lugo >   N-540

O Castro †

Casa Maruja P → **1.3** Castromaior

Xunta Albergue **7.8** → **1** A   **GONZAR**

Casa García **2**   *Café Descanso del Peregrino*

puesta del sol   N

Toxibó

salida del sol

Fábrica

PORTOMARÍN *(Pop. 2,000)*

A **1** O Mirador

0.0 Glorieta

Embalse de Belesar

0.0 km Portomarín from albergue ❶ make your way back down to the main road and over the second (smaller) bridge over the río Torres **[0.4 km]**. We now continue up through dense woodland around St. Anthony's height *alto San Antonio* to join the pilgrim track *senda* by the main road at **San Mamed-Belad [1.8 km]** cross over by *Fábrica de Ladrillos* and re-cross by Coren fertilizer plant in **Toxibo [1.8 km]** after which we have a brief and delightful respite through woodland past *[F.]* to **Gonzar [3.8 km]**.

7.8 km Gonzar popular (busy) *Café Descanso del Peregrino* on the main road and *Alb.* ❶ Gonzar *Xunta.[28÷1]* €6 noisy location on main road but recently refurbished. Around the corner (100m) *Alb.* ❷ **Casa Garcia** *Priv.[30÷5]+* €10–€35 © 982 157 842 traditional village house with covered courtyard (see photo) in quiet location off main road also *Café-menú*.

Continue and turn off <left onto minor road and then right> onto track before joining road into:

1.2 km Castromaior (originally a Celtic castro) *P* **Casa Maruja** © 982 189 054 *Café O Castro* Romanesque church of Santa María. Continue through the village crisscrossing main road and back to:

2.5 km Hospital de la Cruz where the N-540 cuts through this ancient village – its medieval pilgrim hospice no longer visible, but hospitality awaits at *Hs* **El Labrador** €30 © 982 545 303 & restaurant. *Alb.* **Hospital de la Cruz** *Xunta.[32÷1]* €6 another conversion of a school building by the main road (N-540 Ourense – Lugo) take the minor road flyover to the next village:

1.4 km Ventas de Narón *Alb.* ❶ **Casa Molar** *Priv.[18÷2]+* €10-30 © 696 794 507 traditional stone house with restaurant and bar (see photo). *Alb.* ❷ **O Cruceiro** *Priv.*[22÷2]+* €10-30 © 658 064 917 also with restaurant and bar. Tiny stone chapel *Capela de Magdalene* with picnic area adjoining. *[The area was scene of a fierce battle in 840 between Moor and Christian*

but there is nothing here now to disturb the peace beyond pilgrim chatter in the 2 cafés]. Now we start to climb the Sierra Ligonde to the highest point of today's route (720m) passing dog kennels *perreras Alejo* before dropping down to the ancient hamlet of **Lameiro** with the *Antiguo Hospital de Peregrinos* (now a private house – right) and just beyond the ancient *Casa da Carneiro* which provided hospitality to no less than the holy Roman emperor Charles V and King Philip of Spain while on his way to marry Mary Tudor.

3.7 km Ligonde equally ancient hamlet long associated with the camino with its *Cemeterio de Peregrinos* and humble hospitality at *Alb.* ❶ **Fuente del Peregrino** *Priv.[20÷2]* €-donativo © 687 550 527 basic facilities with communal meal prepared by voluntary hospitaleros. ❷ **Escuela de Ligonde** *Muni.[20]* © 679 816 061 skilfully restored hostel with all facilities. *[Ligonde was formerly a significant medieval stop on the way. Charlemagne reputedly stayed here and other royal* *personages and it had a pilgrim hospice]*. Igrexa de Santiago has a Romanesque porch. Opposite the Albergue is a short track down over the río Ligonde passing café-restaurant *Casa Mari Luz* (right) up past church and cruceiro into:

0.6 km Eirexe *Alb.* ❶ **Airexe** *Xunta.[20÷2]* €6 former school building at crossroads with all facilities. To the rear is ❷ **Eirexe** *Priv.[6÷1]+* –€10 ⓒ 982 153 475 with bar-menú. At the crossroads is restaurant *Conde Valdemar*. Continue on quiet country road passing splendid 17th century wayside cross (left) by gnarled oak tree and the ancient hamlet of **Lameiros** with its diminutive capela San Marcos we climb gently to cross of 5 roads with fine views of the surrounding countryside before dropping down into **Portos** *Alb.* A **Paso de Formiga** (Ants Way!) *Priv.[8÷1]+* €10–€25 ⓒ 618 984 605. Continue s/o to:

2.1 km Portos *A Calzada / Detour Alb.* **A Calzada** *Priv.[10÷1]* €10 ⓒ 982 183 744 separate stone pavilion at the rear. No kitchen but meals available at the popular café-restaurant with peaceful garden and picnic area.

Detour: Vilar de Donas ● ● ● ● recommended detour (4.6 km there & back) to this national monument and ancient seat of the Knights of Santiago. Closed Mondays and holidays (check in A Calzada for opening times) The Church of El Salvador is primarily 14th century but its origins go back to the formation of a convent here in the 12th century founded by 2 noble women (hence the appellation Donas). The stone effigies of the knights and its unique frescoes (see photo under reflections) are hauntingly expressive and miraculously well preserved. *Directions:* Turn right off the camino (opposite A Calzada) along quiet country lane across the main road **[1.1 km]** (N-547 Palas de Rei – Lugo) passing rest area *área de descanco* (right) for remaining **[1.2 km]** to:

2.3 km **Vilar de Donas – Igrexa San Salvador**. Take time to soak in its ancient history and to savour its treasures lovingly attended by the knowledgeable guardian. Return the same way.

From *A Calzada* continue along pathways into and through the hamlets of *Lestedo* **[0.6 km]** *CR* Rectoral de Lestedo ⓒ 982 153 435 converted from an original pilgrim hospital, then priests house *casa rectoral* and finally to this modernised gem with rooms from €57. Dinner available. We pass village cemetery and then Valos, Mamurria and on to *A Brea* **[1.8 km]** *Mesón A Brea* on the main N-547. A short woodland path at the back of the restaurant takes us up to *Alto Rosario* **[0.9 km]**. *[Here (before the trees were planted) you could see the sacred peak above Santiago Pico Sacro and on entering the hamlet of Rosario pilgrims would start to recite the Rosary, hence the name]*. We now pass through the hamlet which adjoins the main road before entering the suburbs of Palas de Reis and its delightful municipal parkland **[1.0 km]**:

4.3 km Palas de Rei *Pavillón Alb.* ❶
Os Chacotes *Xunta.[112÷3]* €6 © with 3
cavernous dormitories packed tightly with
bunk beds. The design is so modern they
even invented a new description *Pavillón de
Peregrinos*. Directly opposite is a pilgrim
assistance centre and a more traditional
municipal hostel with basic facilities only.
Here amongst the restful parkland we also

find the *H**** **Complejo La Cabana** © 982 380 750 €35+. with chalet style rooms
and restaurant. Continue past sports stadium into town passing c/Paz (left 50m) to:
❷ **Mesón de Benito** *Priv.[100÷7]* €10 © 982 103 386 modern purpose built hostel
with restaurant *menú* €10. Continue into town taking lane opp. *Café O Cruceiro* and
the parish church of *San Tirso* first built in the 11th century now only retaining its
original Romanesque doorway. *[F.]* Down steps to main road and ❸ **San Marcos**
Priv.[58÷7]+ €10 © 982 380 711 ultra-modern design. Cross road to: ❹ **Castro**
Priv.*[56÷6] €10 © 609 080 655 with bar & restaurant on corner of Av. de Ourense.
❺ **Outeiro** *Priv.[50÷6]* €10 © 982 380 242 m: 630 134 357 new build on c/ Outeiro
off Plaza de Galicia. The camino continues s/o down steps into rua Iglesia and
restaurant *A Forxa* with rear patio *(left)*.

1.2 km Palas de Rei *Centro* ❻ Xunta
[60÷7] €6 original hostel still popular with
pilgrims on account of its central position
located at main road junction directly opp.
Town Hall *Casa Concello* (see photo). Just
over the road on rua do Peregrino (backing
on to praza Concello) is: ❼ **Buen Camino**
Priv.*[41÷8] €8 © 982 380 233 network*
hostel in renovated town house with all

facilities. On the edge of town: ❽ **A Casina di Marcello** *Priv.[17÷2]* €10 © 640
723 903 c/Camiño de abaixo. *[Next albergue: Mato Casanova – 6.3 km].*

❒ **Other accommodation:** *Hr*** **Benilde** © 982 380 717 c/del Mercado. *P** **Casa
Curro** © 982 380 044 Av. Ourense. *P** **Guntina** © 982 380 080 Trav. do Peregrino
(opp. Buen Camino). The main N-547 goes through the town centre as *Av. de
Compostela* on which we find (up town): *Hs** **Vilariño** © 982 380 152 and (down)
P* **Plaza** © 982 380 109 with internet café. ❒ *Turismo* (Oficina Municipal) Av. de
Compostela 28 © 982 380 001. Note the regular Lugo – Santiago bus stops here.

❒ **Palas de Rei** straddles the camino and was a 'compulsory' stop in the *Codex
Calixtinus*. Little remains to remind us of its illustrious past but the name derives
from *Pallatium Regis* palace of the Visigothic king Witiza who reigned from 702
– 710. The Church of **Santiago de Alba** *XII*** has a Romanesque portal and scallop
shell motifs are visible in the town. Today, it is an administrative centre with good
modern facilities serving a population of 3,600 mostly engaged in the dairy industry
and the well known Ulloa cheese. ❒ **Detours** *Share a taxi?*: **Vilar de Donas** built
in the 12th century as a monastic church and linked to the Order of the Knights of
Santiago and the Templars. Tranquil location and stunning frescoes (see photo right).
Pambre Castle one of the finest military castles of its era. Built in the fourteenth
century by Gonzalo Ozores de Ulloa on the Banks of the Pambre river. Check with
the municipal office or try the castle direct © 628 159 469. Alternatively visit from
albergues Casa Domingo or A Bolboreta (see next stage).

REFLECTIONS:

❏ Walking, I am listening to a deeper way... all my ancestors are behind me. *'Be still, they say. Watch and listen. You are the result of the love of thousands'*.

Linda Hogan

03 68.2 km (42.4 ml) – Santiago

PALAS DE REI – RIBADISO (ARZÚA)

⋯⋯⋯⋯	--- ---	18.2	--- ---	71%
▬▬	--- ---	6.6	--- ---	26%
▬▬	--- ---	0.8	--- ---	3%
Total km		**25.6 km**	(15.9 ml)	

▲	--- ---	26.5 km (+ 0.9 km)
Alto ▲		O Coto 515m (1,670 ft)

< 🅰 🄷 > San Xulián **3.5** km – Casanova **5.8** km – O Coto **8.4** km – Melide **14.5** km – Boente **20.3** km – Castañeda **22.5** km.

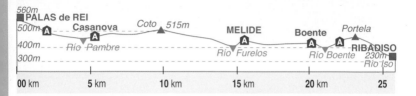

❏ **The Practical Path:** Today we cross 6 shallow river valleys and ¾ on pathways mostly through delightful woodland that helps to stifle the noise from the busy N-547 which we cross and re-cross all the way to Arzúa. Melide makes a good half way stop where we can sample the renowned octopus *pulpo Gallega* and explore the historic old town. Melide is also where pilgrims walking the Camino Primitivo (via Oviedo) join the main camino Francés.

❏ **The Mystical Path:** Will you see the tiny representation of Santiago in the flyover? He appears at the entrance and the exit, welcoming us and blessing us on our way. What does he represent to you and why do we follow his way? Is it to revere his relics that may lie in a silver casket two days ahead? Is that what brought you this far? Do you believe he chose to martyr his earthly body so we could venerate it? He has many names, but who was he really and what significance does he play in our story? What unknown hand beckons us to follow in the way of the true Master? Where will we find Him?

❏ **Personal Journal:** *"... In each moment I sense my guides setting up situations for me to learn the next lesson. I have an image of adoring angels urging me to learn through grace rather than grit. But the lesson will be integrated in perfect timing and with exquisite precision for the exact amount of sand required to produce the pearl. Not one grain too many, but, alas, not one grain too few. So my angelic escort set me up Toshio, just when I had lost my inner way and was confused as to my motivation. And he asks me three questions: each one a reminder of my reason for doing this pilgrimage and an invaluable aid to its accomplishment. How, in heaven's name, did they conceive of a Japanese Shinto grandfather to place on the earthly path of a lost Christian soul? ..."*

Milpes **A** ARZÚA
RIBADISO de Baixo
Los Caminantes **2** **1** Xunta
3.1 ← Puente *río Iso*
N-547
Manuel
Portela
C *Casa Garea*
C ← *Casa Milia*
La Calleja **C**
Albergue **2.2** → **A** Santiago
CASTAÑEDA

río Boente

BOENTE
Cruce **X** **3.3** **2** **1**
Os Albergues **1** *Iglesia Santiago*
El Alemán
Raído
Penas
Carballal

San Lázaro

2.5 Puente

S.María →
Camino Primitivo
Lugo >
AC-840

MELIDE
Sancti Spiriti
5
1.5 Centro *Rotonda*
San Pedro
1 **H** Carlos
FURELOS
4.6 Puente Velha
río Furelos

N-547
*Polígono
Industrial
Gándarra*

Disicabo
Sta.María XIII
Lobreiro *río Seco*
O Coto **2.7**
C Casa de Somoza
CORNIXA

A CORUÑA
LUGO

N-547

Casanova **A** ← **2.3** Albergue

Casa Domingo **A**
Ponte Campaña Mato
Ulloa
N-547
SAN XULIÁN
Albergue **3.4** → **A**
O Abrigadoiro
río Roxán
río Pambre

CARBALLAL
Ponterroxan **P**
F
Centro **0.0** → **6 A** **PALAS de REI**

MELIDE inset

7 Xunta
Apalpador **6** **H** Chiquitín
5 S.Antón
4 Vilela
M **i**
Pereiro **8**
*Pz
Const.*
P Xaneiro
Qinzan
Rua Trek
MELIDE
(Pop. 7,500)
Estilo → **P**
Oroís **P**
parque
3 Cruceiro
P Doronguela
2 Apalpador II
Crucero
S.Roque
Ezequiel **1**
Garnacha **1**
H Carlos
1 Melide
P Xaneiro-II

*Castillo
Pambre*
Ramil
Remonde
A Bolboreta **A**

*puesta
del sol*
O
S
N
E
*salida
del sol*

52

0.0 km Palas de Rei *Centro* albergue ❻ continue over the N-547 down rua do Peregrino and over the N-547 past monument and field of the pilgrims *Campo dos Romeiros* where medieval pilgrims gathered for the journey to Santiago and onto a path to cross the N-547 past *[F.]* and back down to the N-547 with *P* **Ponterroxan** €38 © 982 380 132 and cross the river Ruxián and up into Carballal with its raised granaries *Horreos* back down to re-cross the N-547 again onto woodland path into:

3.4 km San Xulián (*Xiao*) do Camiño classical camino village with its tiny 12th century church dedicated to Saint Julian and *Alb.* **O Abrigadoiro** *Priv.[18÷3]* €10-12 © 676 596 975 with dinner €10 and breakfast available. The path continues down to the Rió Pambre that we cross at Ponte Campaña-Mato **[1.0** km] and *Alb.* **Casa Domingo ♥** *Priv.*[16÷3]* © 982 163 226 network* hostel part of an old mill occupying a tranquil rural setting on the river Pambre with communal dinner. The route now climbs gently through ancient oak woods for **[1.3** km] to Mato-Casonova:

2.3 km Casanova *Alb.* **Mato Casanova** *Xunta.[20÷2]* €6 © the last Xunta hostel in Lugo (see photo) before we enter into A Coruña in this quiet rural location surrounded by woodland (no local facilities). We proceed up the country lane to junction (left) for *off route* (1½ km) the popular albergue and welcoming casa rural **A Bolboreta** *Priv. [8÷2]+* €13 incl. / €27 single / €37 double / Dinner €9. © 609 124 717 a traditional stone house by Vilar de Remonde with possibility to detour to Pambre.

Detour: Castillo de Pambre. From *A Bolboreta* there is a 2½ km (5 km return) designated walk by medieval bridge passing an ancient Celtic Castro to the impressive 14th century Castillo de Pambre. Strategically situated on the río Pambre it has survived the advances of time and the Irmandiños revolt (the war in which the aristocracy were fighting the peasants rather than each other). The fight continues with disputes between private ownership and public access. Unlike its counterpart in Sarria, the four corner towers and inner keep are still proudly standing. 2 km further is the Palacio Villamayor de Ulloa one of the best-preserved Galician manor houses *Pazos*, family seat of the Ulloa's and setting for the novel *Los Pazos de Ulloa* by Emilia Pardo Bazán (only available in Spanish).

Continue up the Pass of the Oxen *Porto de Bois [scene of a bloody battle between warring nobility]* Hotel Pambre Balneario (left) the high point of this stage at 515m before crossing over the provincial border at scrap yard in Cornixa, past *café Campanilla* if busy continue to O Coto (700m).

2.7 km O Coto crossroads hamlet with several *cafés* vying for the breakfast trade. Also *P*** **Los dos Alemanes** €30 © 981 507 337 & *CR* **Casa de Somoza** © 981 507 372 (prior booking). We now follow a delightful undulating track through woods to cross a medieval bridge into the quintessential camino village of *field of hares* **Leboreiro** no facilities but the Romanesque Church of **Santa María [0.8** km] *XIIIth* with fine carved stone tympanum of Virgin and Child over the main door. The house opposite with armorial shield was formerly a pilgrim hostel donated by the Ulloa family. We now cross the medieval Magdalena Bridge over the río Seco into **Disicabo**. The path continues up towards the main road and over a footbridge to join a stretch of senda separating the N-547 from an industrial estate *polígono industrial*

Gándara [F.] Mesón Terra do Melide [**1.6** km]. Here the *Orde de Caballeros y Damas del Camino de Santiago* have erected a monument to themselves and a huge sword of Santiago leads us back through woodland down to **Furelos [2.2** km]:

4.6 km Furelos *Ponte Velha* medieval bridge into Furelos with *Igrexa San Juan*. No trace remains of the medieval pilgrim hospice but a house adj. the church is now a museum. Bar taberna *Farruco [F.]* From here we begin the climb up to Melide through modern suburbs past the first of 6 albergues ❶ **Melide** *Priv.[42÷2]* €10 ✆ 627 901 552 with front entrance on Av.

Lugo. Continue s/o up to join main road opp. the Romanesque Church of *San Pedro & San Roque* beside its famous 14ᵗʰc stone cross reputed to be the oldest in Galicia *Crucero do Melide* – Christ in majesty and Christ crucified on the reverse (see photo). We now make our way up past variety of pulperias and cafes (parque S.Roque left) to *Alb.* ❷ **O Apalpador II** *Priv.[24÷1]* €10 ✆ 981 506 266 m: 679 837 969 Cantón de San Roque, 9 (Concepción Amo also runs O Apalpador on c/ San Antonio). S/0 to busy roundabout *Ronda de la Coruña*.

1.5 km Melide *Centro Alb.* ❸ **O Cruceiro** *Priv.[72÷12]* €10 ✆ 616 764 896 right in the centre on Ronda de A Coruña, 2 with its neo-classical façade and all facilities (incl. a lift to the upper floors!) ● 2 waymarked routes from the central roundabout through the old town as follows: (see map). ❶ Direct route via rua Principal and Plaza Constitución or ❷ via rua Convento to Concello and Turismo (museo) and rua S.Antonio with access to *Alb.* ❹ **Vilela** *Priv.[24÷2]*+ €10 ✆ 616 011 375 c/ San Antonio, 2. ❺ **San Antón** *Priv.[36÷5]* €10 ✆ 981 506 427 m. 698 153 672 c/ San Antón, 6 and at the end of the street (and town) ❻ **O Apalpador** *Priv.[30÷3]* €10 ✆ 679 837 969 c/ San Antonio, 23 and the adj. ❼ **Melide** *Xunta.[156÷7]* €6 with all modern facilities in its cavernous interior (recently refurbished). Finally on c/Progreso, 43 we find *Alb* ❽ **Pereiro** *Priv.[45÷4]* €10 ✆ 981 506 314. **Other Accommodation:** *H*⁺⁺**Carlos** ✆ 981 507 633 lower end of Av. Lugo (adj. albergue 1). *Hs*⁺⁺**Xaneiro II** ✆ 981 506 140 Av. de la Habana. *P*⁺ Orois ✆ 981 506 140 rua A.Bóvena. *P*⁺ **Berenguela** ✆ 981 505 417 off r/S.Roque. *P*⁺Estilo c/del Progreso. Opp. Xunta albergue *Pousada* **Chiquitín** €30+ ✆ 981 815 333 Rúa San Antón, 18 ultra modern with restaurant & roof terrace to the rear.

MELIDE: *Turismo* (9:00-15:00) Plaza Convento ✆ 981 505 003 Casa Concello and administrative centre with (declining) population of 7,500. The old part follows its medieval layout of narrow winding streets with shops, bars and restaurants serving the regional speciality, octopus *pulpo*. For a local experience try *pulpería Garnacha* or *Exequiel* on Av.de Lugo. In *Plaza del Convento* we find the austere parish church, Sancti Spiritus, formerly a 14ᵗʰc Augustinian monastery. Opp. is the original pilgrim refuge of 1502 *Antigo Hospital de Peregrinos* now a museum and Tourist information centre. Melide remains an important hub of the Jacobean pilgrimage and the point where pilgrims travelling down from Oviedo on the original pilgrim route *camino Primitivo* join the *camino Francés*. Today's pilgrim facilities include a •*Masaje y fisioterapia* (servicio al peregrino) in c/Lavadoiro,18 ✆ 981 507 017 and pilgrim hiking gear at •*Rua Trekking* ✆ 981 507 017 r/Convento (near popular restaurant *Casa Qinzan*).

We leave Melida via the western suburbs past *cementerio* [**0.4** km] over N-547 (sign San Martiño) past Romanesque *Igrexa Santa María de Melide XII* [**0.6** km] at which point we leave the busyness of Melide behind and make our way into woodland to **arroyo San Lázaro** [1.5 km] (the ruins of the leprosy hospice long disappeared).

2.5 km **Puente río San Lázaro** we cross this small river via a stone causeway *[We cross several shallow river valleys during these final stages so our path is more undulating than the contour guide might suggest. Ultreya!]* Our way is now by path that winds through shaded forest, oak and chestnut increasingly giving way to eucalyptus and pine. Continue through Carballal and the river beyond [1.6 km] through Parabispo over the río Raído with picnic area [2.2 km] passing Peroxa and café *El Alemán* down to the N-547 [1.1 km] at:

3.3 km **Boente** *Cruce Igrexa Santiago* with image of the Saint above the altar and convivial parish priest who offers a blessing to passing pilgrims. The hostels fronting the main road don't share the same positivity. *Alb.* ❶ **Os Albergues** *Priv. [28÷7]* €11 ℂ 981 501 853 + *Os Mesón* bar menú. ❷ **Boente** *Priv.[22÷5]* ℂ 981 501 974 + menú. We leave past Cruceiro and *[F.]* through underpass down into the Boente valley with shaded rest area (right) the delightful riverside setting somewhat marred by the noise of traffic. Up the other side we join minor road (N-547 in a cutting below) into Castañeda past café *No Camino* and the parish Church of Santa María to:

2.2 km **Castañeda** *Alb.* **Santiago** *Priv. [4÷1]+* €10 +35 ℂ 981 501 711 prominently located on the corner *A Fraga Alta* with attractive terrace bar and restaurant. *[It was here in Castañeda that the pilgrims would deposit the limestone rocks they had brought from Triacastela to be fired for the lime used in the building of the Cathedral at Santiago].* Just beyond the albergue we pass

casa rural *CR* **La Calleja** ℂ 605 787 382 with rooms from €25 and down over river with shaded rest area [0.6 km]. From here we go around a wooded hill with track (right) *[leads to N-547 and casa rurales 400m off route: Garea €35-40 ℂ 981 500 400 and Milía ℂ 981 515 241].* We now climb to alto (440m) and cross a raised pass over the N-547 [1.0 km] through woodland to pick up minor road with café-bar *Manuel* [0.6 km] down to the beautiful medieval bridge over the río Iso [0.3 km] at:

3.1 km **Ribadiso da Baixo** *Alb.* ❶ **Ribadiso** *Xunta.[70÷3]* €6 ℂ idyllic location right on the river Iso adjoining the medieval bridge. All facilities with toilets in a separate block to the rear. Pleasant space to relax on the river bank (weather permitting). This is a wonderful reconstruction of one of the oldest pilgrim hospitals still in existence with an award for environmental architecture. Adjoining bar and restaurant and *Alb.* ❷ **Los Caminantes**

Priv.[52÷3]+ €10-38 (double room) ℂ 647 020 600. *Alb.*❸ **Milpes** *Priv.[38÷3]* €10 ℂ 981 500 425 m: 616 652 276 with welcoming bar and splendid views of the surrounding countryside. Also *off route* modern *CR* **Vaamonde** ℂ 981 500 364 in Traserexe. *[Next albergue: Arzúa – 2.0 km].*

REFLECTIONS:

❑ **Let no one come to you without leaving better and happier.** *Mother Teresa*

04 **42.6** km (26.5 ml) – Santiago

RIBADISO – PEDROUZO *(ARCA / O PINO)*

⦙⦙⦙⦙⦙⦙⦙⦙⦙⦙⦙	--- ---	12.2	--- ---	54%
▬▬▬▬	--- ---	8.2	--- ---	36%
▬▬▬	--- ---	2.4	--- ---	10%
Total km		**22.8 km**	(13.9 ml)	

◣◥◤ --- --- 23.6 km (^160m + 0.8 km)

Alto ▲ Santa Irene 405m (1,328 ft)

< **Ⓐ Ⓗ** > Arzúa **3.2** km – Salceda 14.4 – Santa Irene **19.6** km – A Rua **21.0** km.

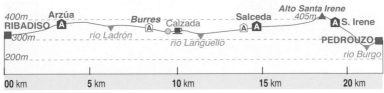

❑ **The Practical Path:** over ½ this stage is on natural pathways with good shade offered by the ubiquitous eucalyptus. We start with a steep climb up into Arzúa and end with a gentle climb around the alto de Santa Irene. In between we have a largely level path with just 3 shallow river valleys.

❑ **The Mystical Path:** The beautiful memorial to Guillermo Watt is timely. What plans have *we* made for our onward journey? Or are we too preoccupied with the dramas of this life to consider the next? To contemplate the impermanence of our earthly form can be revitalising, urging us to make every step a prayer for understanding, every breath a song of gratitude, every moment a chance to awaken from the dream that keeps us separate from our eternal Source.

❑ **Personal Reflections:** *"… The debate became heated, the only seeming accord being that the problems that beset our world were real and worsening. She had remained silent but now took the rare moment of quiet to state with utter conviction, 'There is only one solution'. Her words made us attentive – 'Allah'. The response was so unexpected. We had been looking for solutions on the level of the problem – our human condition of fear. She was a Sufi devotee. I laugh at the paradox that it took a Muslim woman walking an outwardly Christian path to point out to us the deeper truth that lay beyond. Whatever name we choose to describe the ineffable is immaterial. The only way out of our dilemma, is inward through Love …"*

0.0 km **Ribadiso** from the albergues proceed up to and through the tunnel under the N-547 and veer right> on the far side past *Alb.* **Milpes** (previous page) back onto track parallel to the main road which we follow all the way into **Arzua** *suburbs* **[1.8 km]** passing *Pr*** **Retiro** €48 ✆ 981 500 554 Av. de Lugo and the latest **albergue [0.6 km]** *Alb.* ❶ **de Selmo** *Priv.[50÷1]* €10 ✆ 981 939 018 ✆ Av. de Lugo, 133. opp. *P**Rua ✆ 981 500 139 next *Alb.* ❷ **Don Quijote** *Priv.*[50÷1]* €10 ✆ 981 500 139 modern terraced building adj. ❸ **Ultreia** *Priv.*[38÷2]* €10 ✆ 981 500 471 another network* hostel in same modern block with all facilities and café. Directly opp. ❹

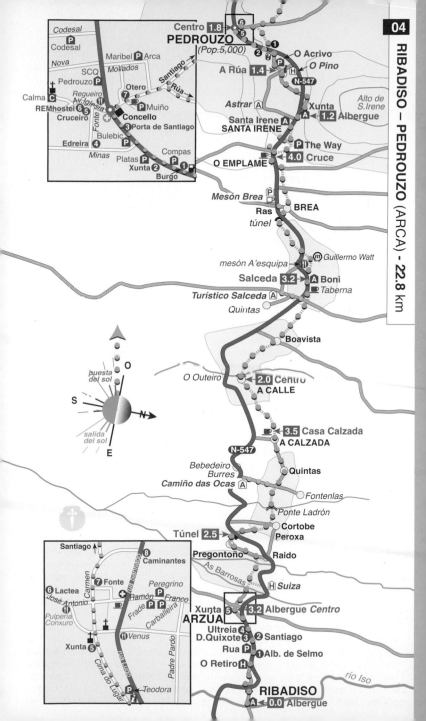

Codesal
P
Codesal
Nova
Maribel P Arca
SCQ **Mollados**
Pedrouzo P
Calma C Otero P
+ **Regueiro** 7
REMhostel 6 Av.Iglesia
Cruceiro 5 P Muiño
Bulebic 3 Porta de Santiago
Edreira 4 **Minas**
Platas P
Xunta 2 P
Burgo 1
Compas

Centro 1.8
PEDROUZO
(Pop:5,000)
6
5
1
A Rúa 1.4 2 O Acrivo
P O Pino
H
N-547
Astrar A
Santa Irene A Xunta
SANTA IRENE A 1.2 Albergue
P **The Way**
O EMPLAME 4.0 Cruce
Mesón Brea P
BREA
Ras
túnel
m Guillermo Watt
mesón A'esquipa
Salceda 3.2 A Boni
Turístico Salceda A P Taberna
Quintas
Boavista
O Outeiro 2.0 **Centro**
A CALLE
3.5 Casa Calzada
A CALZADA
Bebedeiro
Burres Quintas
Camiño das Ocas A
Fontenlas
Ponte Ladrón
Cortobe
Peroxa
Túnel 2.5
Pregontoño Raido
As Barrosas
H Suiza
Xunta 5 3.2 Albergue **Centro**
Ultreia 4
D.Quixote 3 2 Santiago
Rua P 1 Alb. de Selmo
O Retiro H
RIBADISO
A 0.0 Albergue
río Iso

O
puesta
del sol
S N
salida
del sol
E

Santiago
8
Caminantes
6 Lactea 7 Fonte
José-Antonio **Peregrino**
Pulpería Ramón P
Conxuro Frade Franco
Carballeira
Xunta 5 H Venus
Cima do Lugar
Teodora
7 P

Santiago Apostol *Priv.[72÷3]* €10 © 981 508 132 all mod cons + lift! café with pilgrim menú. Proceed towards the centre of town and the **Plaza Mayor [0.6 km]** *Turismo* adj. *P°°* **Teodora** © 981 500 083 with popular restaurant. Turn <left into rúa Cima do Lugar and adj. *Iglesia de Santiago y capela da Madalena* [0.2 km]:

3.2 km Arzúa *Alb.* ❺ **Arzúa** *Xunta [46÷2]* €6 © 660 396 824 restored town house in central location with all facilities. 50m beyond we come to a crossroads with alt. albergues (all within a few hundred meters) compete for the lucrative pilgrim trade. Turn left for ❻ **Vía Láctea** *Priv.[120÷10]* €10 © 981 500 581 rua José Antonio (just beyond pulperia *O Conxuro*).

The camino continues s/o down rúa do Carmen with the traditional ❼ **da Fonte** *Priv.[20÷5]* €10-12 © 981 501 118 Rúa do Carme, 18 a quiet 'backwater'. Continue up to the right to the main road Av. de Lugo (N-547) for: ❽ **Los Caminantes II** *Priv.[28÷1]* €10 © 647 020 600 all facilities . **Other Lodging:** *Central P°* **Casa Frade** © 981 500 019 rúa Ramón Franco and adj. *P°* **Casa Carballeira** © 981 500 094 opp. *Hs°* **Mesón do Peregrino** © 981 500 830. Further out the modern *H°°* **Suiza** © 981 500 862 on the main road N-547.

ARZÚA *Turismo* Praza do Peregrino © 981 508 056. The the last major centre of population (6,300) before we enter Santiago. The untidy development of the modern town is mirrored in the haphazard layout of the older central part and waymarking is also irregular. Off the central square (with variety of bars, cafés and restaurants) is the modern parish church dedicated to St. James with image of Santiago as both Moorslayer and pilgrim and just behind is the original 14th century Augustinian *Capilla de La Magdalena*. The town is known for its local cheese and the cheese fair *festa do queixo* held in March. The camino continues out through the old quarter of town down c/del Carmen (left of the main road) past fountain and over stream (site of San Lázaro hospice) onto a delightful track through ancient oak woods in *As Barrosas* (track to Hotel Suiza right) meandering over several small streams onto side road into Preguntoño to take path under the N-547:

2.5 km N-547 **túnel** we now alternate between country lanes & track bypassing the hamlets of **Raído**, **Fondevila**, **Cortobe**, and just beyond **Taberna Velha** *[½ km detour to: Alb.* **Camiño das Ocas** *Priv.[28÷5]+* €10 © 648 404 780 on the N-547 in Burres].* Continue over rio Ladrón into:

3.5 km A **Calzada** *Casa Calzada* popular track side café. Continue into:

2.0 km A **Calle** quaint village with traditional houses (cafe *Tia* adj. the river currently closed/for sale). The camino wends its way over the stream through **Boavista** and shortly afterwards at a crossroads ✣ is detour to: *[Alb.* **turístico Salceda** *Priv.[8÷1]+* €12-40 © 981 502 767 + bar/menú V. ½ km the **far** side of the N-547].* The camino continues s/o down to the N-547 at:

3.2 km **Salceda** on the N-547 with bar *Taberna Salceda* and *Alb.* **Bondi** *Priv. [30÷6]* €10 © 618 965 907. *Mesón A'esquipa / Bar Verde* with outdoor rest area. Continue on woodland path with monument (right) to pilgrim *Guillermo Watt* who died at this spot only a day away from his earthly destination. Take care as we crisscross the N-547 [!] into *Ras* where a pedestrian underpass *túnel* [2.0 km] brings us safely into **Brea [0.4** km] detour: ❖ *[left 100m far side of N-547 P Mesón Brea Bar S.Miguel © 981 511 040].* ❖ Continue s/o and back over the N-547 past 'rest' area up to crossroads **[1.6 km].**

4.0 km Cruce *O Empalme O Ceadoiro* menú. Cross N-547 onto track through woods around *Alto de Santa Irene*. *P* The Way €12-15 en suite €45 © 628 120 202 Brea No 36. Continue down past *túnel* **[0.8** km] ❖ *[Detour to* ❶ *Alb.* **Santa Irene** *Priv.* [15÷2]* €13 © 981 511 000 network* hostel (see photo) rear garden & menú* €13. *Adj. capela Santa Irene (an early Christian martyr). 700m further on off route:* ❷ *Alb.* **Rural Astar** *Priv.[24÷2]* €10 © 981 511 463 m: 608 092 820.   Continue s/o past pilgrim rest area [F.] **[0.4 km]** to:

1.2 km Santa Irene *Alb.* ❸ **Santa Irene** *Xunta.[32÷2]* all facilities but directly on the busy main road (noisy). Continue down on woodland path through *túnel* **[0.8** km] down into *A Rúa* **[0.6** km]:

1.4 km A Rúa traditional hamlet with *Turismo Asoc. Hostelería Compostela* © 696 652 564 who provide general info. from Easter-Oct. and can pre-book hotels in Santiago. *[Just off route signposted (200m) H* O Pino © 981 511 035 on main road]. CR* **Casa Gallega** © 981 511 463 opp. *CR* **O Acivro** single from €35 © 981 511 316 m: 609 105 948 with restful bar /restaurant and extensive garden. Continue over rio Burgo to climb steeply up to N-547 **opción [0.6** km]: Two options to access O Pedrouzo: ❷ turn left along the busy main road to *Alb.* ❶ *(Concello 1.0 km) or* ❶ take the recommended woodland access leading to the rear of the town and *Alb.* ❼ *(Concello 1.2 km).* For this latter route continue s/o over the N-547 onto woodland path merging into rua peregrino past Cultural/Sports hall to T-Junction *[waymarked path to Santiago turns right].* To access accommodation in Pedrouzo 200m turn <left into rua Concello passing the delightful *P* O Muiño* (Mayka) © 686 419 046 with quiet garden to rear adj. *bar O Muiño* and *Alb.* ❼ **Otero** *Priv.[36÷2]* © 671 663 374 on c/Forcarei, 2. Continue s/o to Concello and centre of Pedrouzo:

1.8 km Pedrouzo *Centro Pedrouzo* (town), *Arca* (parish) *O Pino* (municipality) satellite of Santiago straddling the busy N-547 with variety of shops and restaurants. *Note: If you intend to make the Cathedral for 12 noon pilgrim mass you need to leave early in the morning.* Wide range of accommodation mostly on the N-547 (see map). 7 albergues (Xunta €6 others €10) as follows: ❶ **O Burgo** *Priv.*[14÷1]*+ © 630 404 138 on main road with bar adj. gasolinera Repsol. ❷ **Arca** *Xunta.[120÷4]* purpose-built hostel *('tucked' down behind the supermercado off the N-457).* Further on in the town centre ❸ **Porta de Santiago** *Priv.*[56÷3]* © 981 511 103 modern building with café and rear patio. Corner of rua Minas and c/Rua Fonte ❹ **Edreira** *Priv.*[48÷4]* © 981 511 365 purpose-built network* hostel. At the other end of rua Fonte in Av. de la Iglesia, 7 in modern block of apartments: ❺ **Cruceiro** *Priv.[94÷8]* © 981 511 371 facilities incl. sauna. Adj.❻ **REMhostel** *Priv.[40÷1]* © 981 510 407. **Other Lodging** €25-45: *Central* on N-547: *Hs*** **Plantas** © 981 511 378 adj. *P** **BuleBic** © 981 511 222. *Further out*: *P** **Pedrouzo** © 981 510 483 *P* **En Ruta SCQ** © 981 511 471 Av. de Santiago, 23. *P**C**odesal** © 981 511 064 rua Codesal. *P** **Maruja** © 981 511 406 rua Nova adj. parish church on rua Igrexa *P** **Casal de Calma** © 689 910 676. Near O Muiño (entrance/exit) on rua Mollados: *Pr** **Maribel** © 609 459 966 adj. *P* **Arca** © 657 888 594.

❐ He went up into the mountain to pray... and the fashion of his countenance was altered, and his raiment was white and glistening. *Luke IX, 29.*

---

05 **19.8** km (12.3 ml) – Santiago

PEDROUZO (ARCA) – SANTIAGO

....	--- ---	8.0	--- ---	*40%*
▬▬▬▬	--- ---	7.4	--- ---	*38%*
▬▬▬▬	--- ---	<u>4.4</u>	--- ---	*22%*
Total km		**19.8 km**	(12.3 ml)	

◣◣ --- --- 20.4 km (0.6 km)
Alto ▲ Monte do Gozo 370m (1,214 ft)
< Ⓐ Ⓗ > Amenal **3.5** km – Labacolla **9.6** –
Vilamaior **11.0** km – Monte do Gozo **15.3** km – San Lázaro **17.3** km.

❐ **The Practical Path:** The first part of this final stage is through the dense and ever-present eucalyptus. Make the most of their shade and the peace they exude. As we get nearer the city, asphalt and crowds begin to take over as busloads of pilgrims join the route for this one-day into Santiago. If you are making for the pilgrim mass at 12 noon be prepared for large crowds and try and create an air of compassionate detachment – be patient and prepare for the long slog up to Monte Gozo which, while surrounded by woodland, is all on asphalt.

❐ **The Mystical Path:** Will you stay awhile and lose yourself in the tiny grove of holm oak, itself almost lost amongst the mass of alien eucalyptus? Will you stop in Lavacolla, whose waters were used in the ritual cleansing of pilgrims prior to entering the holy City? Today the water is putrid but it is the symbolic purification that we seek so that we might glisten with the pure white light of Christ consciousness.

❐ **Personal Reflections:** *"... I had walked the equivalent of one day for each year Christ spent on earth. Here I was on the 33rd day but I could find no joy on this hill amongst the crowds huddled against the driving rain ... As I entered the cathedral I realised I had failed in my purpose. But in that same instant I realised I had been searching in the wrong place. A sudden rush of joy enveloped my soaking body. I knew the answer lay where the world of things ended and the unseen world began and I knew I had to go there. I hurried down the steps and out the city. I was alone but I had company. I did not know where I was going but I felt completely guided ..."*

0.0 km Pedrouzo *Centro* Turn up rua Concello past albergue ❻ and sports hall *polideportivo* **[0.5 km]** *(the waymarked camino joins from the right).* S/o past bar *Mirás* and <left into dense eucalyptus forest through San Antón down into the río Amenal valley over rio Xeimar and under N-547 *túnel* **[3.0 km]:**

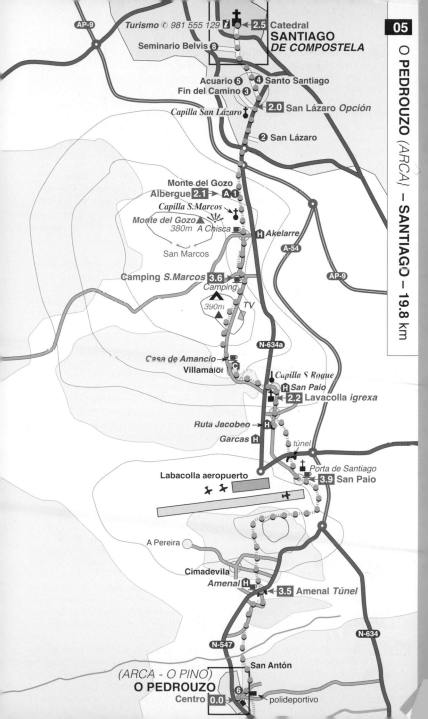

Turismo © 981 555 129 **i**   **2.5** Catedral
SANTIAGO
DE COMPOSTELA

Seminario Belvis **8**

Acuario **5**   **4** Santo Santiago
Fin del Camino **3**
Capilla San Lázaro   **2.0** San Lázaro *Opción*

2 San Lázaro

Monte del Gozo
Albergue **2.1** → **A 1**
Capilla S.Marcos
Monte del Gozo ▲
380m A Chisca   **H** *Akelarre*

San Marcos   A-54

AP-9

Camping *S.Marcos* **3.6**
Camping ▲
390m   TV

N-634a

Casa de Amancio →
Villamaior

Capilla S Roque
H *San Paio*
2.2 Lavacolla *igrexa*

Ruta Jacobeo → **H**
Garcas **H**

túnel

Labacolla aeropuerto   *Porta de Santiago*
✈ ✈   **3.9** San Paio

A Pereira ○

Cimadevila
Amenal **H**
3.5 Amenal *Túnel*

N-547   N-634

San Antón
(ARCA - O PINO)
O PEDROUZO
Centro **0.0**   **6**   polideportivo

3.5 km Amenal *túnel H*°° Amenal © 981 510 431 with popular *Café*. S/o up woodland path through Cimadevila. A wide forest track brings us around the perimeter of Santiago airport to roundabout. A dedicated pilgrim track alongside the motorway takes us down into a deep cutting at the end of the runway (see photo) to cross over an access road into:

3.9 km San Paio ancient hamlet with bar/restaurant *Casa Porta de Santiago*. We now enter the last recognisable stretch of the medieval 'Royal Way' *Real Camino* as we head uphill veering right> onto a natural path lined with remnants of the native deciduous woodland that once covered this area before eucalyptus was imported to fuel the pulp industry. Head downhill passing rear entrance to *H*°°° **Ruta Jacobea** © 981 888 211 (special pilgrim price) to:

2.2 km Lavacolla *Igrexa P*° San Paio © 981 888 205. Lavacolla is recognised today more for the name of the international airport than the place where medieval pilgrims came to wash *lavar* and purify themselves before entering the city. Modern Lavacolla now caters more for the business traveller than the pilgrim with variety of restaurants, bars and hotel. *[Short detour ● ● ● ● Capela San Roque (300m): If you continue down the steps past the bandstand you come to the little chapel dedicated to the pilgrim saint San Roque. While it may be closed it has a covered portico and sits in a shaded grove of trees where you can perform your own purification ritual in relative peace].* The path now continues around the side of the parish church to cross over the access road to the airport (N-634a) and over a small stream to head steeply uphill on dedicated track through crossroads at **Villamaior [1.4** km]: *CR & Café* **Casa de Amancio** © 981 897 086. Continue on pilgrim track down over a stream with rest area and up to our high point today at 396m *[not Monte de Gozo but the studios of Radio TV Galicia! A sign, perhaps, of how TV has come to dominate our lives].* Turn <left at T-jct *Camping San Marcos & Café* **[2.2** km]:

3.6 km Camping *San Marcos*. Continue down side of RTVE into **San Marcos** with several *bars* and *cafés*. *[200m off route s/o H*° **Akelarre** © *981 552 689 on the N-634].* Turn <left up rua San Marcos past *Café A Chica* and a short paved path brings us to the enchanting **capilla de San Marcos** in a glade of trees with *Cantina* and where, if it was not raining, medieval pilgrims espied the cathedral towers (the frist one being crowned

'king' for the day) and giving rise to an exclamation, *'Monte do Gozo / Mount of Joy'*. Today, a monument to the visit of Pope John Paul II and Francis of Assisi stands sentinel atop the hill along with a statue of 2 pilgrims looking towards the cathedral now largely hidden by the sprawling suburbs of Santiago. Continue s/o downhill to:

2.1 km Monte del Gozo *Alb.* ❶ **Monte do Gozo** *Xunta.[400+]* prominently located on this elevated site overlooking the city. 400 beds in separate blockhouses containing rooms with 8 beds in each. Good modern facilities with *bar, restaurant* and large canteen on the main plaza. The hill itself has been reshaped by the bulldozer to provide a vast leisure complex for the city. The sprawling dormitory and recreational buildings are the price of an ever-increasing demand for accommodation. The tiny chapel of San Marcos is the only thing left on the hill that gives any sense of history to this romantic sounding place. The route continues down the hill along Rua do Peregrino and down a flight of steps where we join the city traffic to pass over railway line and past statue of *El Templario Peregrino* (left) over A-9 autopista and roundabout into the wide N-634 and the modern city suburbs with prominent monument to notable historical figures connected with the camino (see photo). At the **2nd roundabout [1.3 km]** on opp. side of the road behind *Museo Pedagóxico Alb.* ❷ **Residencia de Peregrinos San Lázaro** *Xunta.[80÷6]* €10 (€7 subsequent nights) ✆ 981 571 488 all facilities with garden area. Continue along the main road passing *H°* **San Jacobo** ✆ 981 580 361 over busy roundabout to pass the ancient chapel of *San Lázaro Santiago* **[0.6 km]** *[witness to the leprosarium that existed here in the 12th century, sufficiently far outside the*

medieval city walls to ensure contamination didn't spread inside]. 100m later we come to major crossroads (ruas S. Lázaro & Roma) and albergue option **[0.1 km]**

2.0 km San Lázaro *opción Albergues 3 pilgrim hostels lie within 300m and provide an opportunity to unload backpacks and shower before visiting the city. (200m left signposted)* ❸ **Fin del Camino** *(Jaime García Rodríguez) Asoc.[110÷6]* €8 ✆ 981 587 324 junction of r/Roma & c/Moscú, modern building behind the austere *Policía Autonómica* on corner of ruas Moscú and Estocolmo. What it lacks in character it makes up for in the range of shower and laundry facilities and rear patio *(bus 11 to Plaza Galicia).*   Continue s/o into rua do Valiño **[0.3 km]** to ❹ **Santo Santiago** *Priv.[40÷3]* €10 ✆ 657 402 403 with all facilities and restaurant. Below the *parque* (steep steps left): ❺ **Acuario** *Priv.*[60÷9]* Rúa Estocolmo, 2-b. ✆ 981 575 438. Continue into rúa das Fontiñas and Fonte dos Concheiros and over ring road *Av. de Lugo* **[0.8 km]** (main bus station *estación de autobuses* – up right) and enter *Rúa dos Concheiros* named after the stallholders who used to sell pilgrim shells *conchas.* Continue up to N°36 (left) **[0.2 km]** ❻ **La Estrella** *Priv.[24÷1]* €10 ✆ 881 973 926 and just beyond **[0.1 km]** N°10 ❼ **Porta Real** *Priv.[24÷9]* €10-15 ✆ 633 610 114. Continue to the top and St. Peter's cross *Cruceiro de San Pedro* **[0.1 km]** which heralds our arrival into the old city with the spires of the Cathedral ahead.

Option: go direct to main pilgrim hostel at Belvís 500m to our left *(signposted).* Access from the city centre is via rua Trompas (see city plan) ❽ **Seminario Menor La Asunción** *Conv.[177]+* €10-13 ✆ 881 031 768 Av. Quiroga Palacios. Depending on your time of arrival and intentions for the day you might consider going directly to the hostel (opens from 13.30 with lockers for backpacks) *Directions*: Turn left and immediately right into rua dos Lagartos to join alt. route (from

Praza da San Pedro) and continue around the walls of the convento de Belvís to the Seminario Menor which houses the main city hostel (Parque Belvís below).

Continue down rua de San Pedro past the Church of San Pedro & Praza (left) and s/o to the famous Gate of the Way *Porta do Camiño* **[0.4 km]** which gives access to the wonderful old medieval city. Up on the right overlooking the **Porta do Camiño** *Convento de Santo Domingo de Bonaval* housing the Pantheón and Galician museum, with the centre for contemporary Galician art opp. There is a quiet park behind the convent buildings to refresh body and soul from the rigours of city life. (See city map for directions to these and other places of interest). We now proceed up Casas Reais and Rúa das Ánimas into Praza de Cervantes (with statue of the writer atop the central pillar) now we head down rúa da Azabachería (lined with jewellers selling jet *azabache* – see later) into Praza da Inmaculada (also called Azabachería) down under the arch of the **Pazo do Xelmírez [0.3** km] to:

2.5 km　**Praza Obradoiro** *Catedral*. Take time to *arrive*. We each experience different emotions on seeing the Cathedral from euphoria to disappointment. Whatever your individual reaction, honour and accept it. Gratitude for safe arrival is a frequent response but if you are overwhelmed by the crowds why not return later when you feel more composed and the Cathedral is, perhaps, quieter (open daily from 07:00 until 21:00). Whether now or later and whichever door you entered by, you might like to follow the time-worn pilgrim ritual as follows:

[1] Due to erosion it is no longer permitted to place your hand in the Tree of Jesse, the central column of the Master Mateo's masterpiece Door of Glory *Portico de Gloria*. But you can stop and admire the incomparable beauty of this inner portico carved between 1166 and 1188 (the exterior façade was added in 1750). The Bible and its main characters come alive in this remarkable storybook in stone. The central column has Christ in Glory flanked by the apostles and, directly underneath, St. James sits as intercessor between Christ and the pilgrim. Millions of pilgrims over the centuries have worn finger holes in the solid marble as a mark of gratitude for their safe arrival (the reason why it is now protected by a barrier). Proceed to the other side and **[2]** touch your brow to that of Maestro
Mateo whose kneeling figure is carved into the back of the central column (facing the altar) and receive some of his artistic genius in the ritual known as head-butting the saint *Santo d'os Croques* – touch your forehead to his and receive some of his inspiration. Proceed to the High Altar (right) to ascend the stairs and **[3]** hug the Apostle. Perhaps lay your head on his broad shoulders and say what you came here to say. Proceed down the steps on the far side to the crypt and the reliquary chapel under the altar. **[4]** Here, you can kneel before the casket containing the relics of the great Saint and offer your prayer …

　　Pilgrim mass at 12 noon each day (doors may close 5 minutes before on busy days). The swinging of the giant incense burner *Botafumeiro* was originally used to fumigate the sweaty (and possibly disease-ridden) pilgrims. The ritual requires half a dozen attendants *tiraboleiros* to perform it so became an infrequent event but is used increasingly during mass these days. The seating capacity was extended in recent years from 700 to 1,000 so you might even find somewhere to sit but don't hold any expectations and remember – time itself is a journey.

REFLECTIONS: 'Time is the journey from ignorance to Gnosis. Time is imperfection longing to be the Good and progressively improving. Time is the relative reaching towards the Absolute.' *Jesus and the Lost Goddess.*' Freke.

_____

_____

_____

_____

_____

_____

_____

_____

_____

_____

_____

_____

_____

4 squares surround the cathedral and provide access to it, as follows:

■ **Praza do Obradoiro**. The 'golden' square of Santiago is usually thronged with pilgrims and tourists admiring the dramatic west facing façade of the Cathedral, universal symbol of Santiago, with St. James looking down on all the activity from his niche in the central tower. This provides the main entrance to the Cathedral and the Portico de Gloria. To the right of the steps is the discrete entrance to the museum. A combined ticket will provide access to all rooms including the crypt and the cloisters and also to the 12th century palace of one of Santiago's most famous individuals and first archbishop, Gelmírez *Pazo de Xelmírez* situated on the (left). In this square we also find the beautiful Renaissance façade of the Parador named after Ferdinand and Isabel *Hostal dos Reis Católicos* on whose orders it was built in 1492 as a pilgrim hospice. Opposite the Cathedral is the more austere neoclassical seat of the Galician government and town hall *Pazo de Raxoi* with its solid arcade. Finally, making up the fourth side of the square is the gable end of the *Colegio de S. Jerónimo* part of the university. Moving anti-clockwise around the cathedral – turn up into Rúa de Fonseca to:

■ **Praza das Praterías**. The most intimate of the squares with its lovely centrepiece, an ornate statue of horses leaping out of the water. On the corner of Rúa do Vilar we find the Dean's House *Casa do Deán* now the **pilgrim office.** Along the walls of the Cathedral itself are the silversmith's *prateros* that give the square its name. Up the steep flight of steps we come to the magnificent southern door to the Cathedral, the oldest extant doorway and traditionally the entrance taken by pilgrims coming from Portugal. The quality of the carvings and their arrangement is remarkable and amongst the many sculptured figures is one of St. James between two cypress trees. Continuing around to the right we come to:

■ **Praza da Quintana.** This wide square is identified by the broad sweep of steps separating the lower part *Quintana of the dead* from the upper *Quintana of the living*. Opp the Cathedral is the wall of the *Mosteiro de San Paio de Antealtares* (with museum of sacred art). The square provides the eastern entrance to the Cathedral via the Holy Gate *Porta Santa* sometime referred to as the Door of Pardon *El Perdón* only opened during Holy Years (the next in 2021). Adjoining it is the main entrance to the Cathedral shop that has

several guidebooks (in various languages) with details of the Cathedral's many chapels and their interesting carvings and statuary and the priceless artefacts and treasures in the museum. Finally, we head up the broad flight of steps around the corner and back into:

■ **Praza da Inmaculada (Azabachería)** to the north facing Azabachería façade, with the least well-known doorway and the only one that *descends* to enter the Cathedral. It has the most weathered aspect, with moss and lichen covering its bleak exterior. Opposite the cathedral is the imposing southern edifice of *Mosteiro de San Martiño Pinario* the square in front gets any available sun and attracts street artists. The archbishop's arch *Arco Arzobispal* brings us back to the Praza do Obradoiro.

Check in at the •**Pilgrim Office** *Oficina del Peregrino* and welcome centre on rua Vilar, 3/1 adj. the Cathedral ℰ 981 568 846 open daily 09:00-21:00 (10:00-20:00 winter). The office issues the *compostela* and welcomes pilgrims with teams of *Amigos* an initiative of the Irish Society and the CSJ in London who offer help with queries. Here we also find toilets and backpack storage to facilitate unencumbered exploration of the city and a notice board for pilgrim messages. Providing you have fulfilled the criteria of a bona-fide pilgrim and walked at least the last 100 km (200 km on bike or horseback) for religious / spiritual reasons and collected 2 stamps per day on your credencial you will be awarded a certificate of completion *Compostela*. This may entitle you to certain

privileges such as reduced entry fees to museums and discounted travel home and a free meal at the Parador. Another pilgrim welcome centre and place of reflection *Pilgrim House* rua Nova,19 opened in 2014 under the care of Faith and Nath Walter & volunteers from Terra Nova and the USA.

68

❏ **Turismo:** ❖ r/Vilar, 63 © 981-555 129 *June-Sept 09-21 / Oct-May 10-15 & 17-20.*
❖ *Kiosco* Plaza do Galicia. ❖ *TurGalicia* r/do Vilar.43 © 981 584 081.

❏ *Albergues:* ❶ – ❽ (see previous pages. €–*depending on season)* ❾● **La Salle** *Priv.*
[84÷10] €17-19 c/de Tras de Santa Clara© 981 584 611. **10●** **Meiga Backpackers**
Priv.[30÷5] €10-13 c/Basquiños, 67 with garden. © 981 570 846. **11●** **O Fogar de**
Teodomiro *Priv.[20÷5]* €15+ Plaza Algalia de Arriba,3 © 981 582 920. **12●** **The**
Last Stamp *Priv.[62÷10]* €12-18 r/Preguntorio,10. © 981 563 525. **13●** **Azabache**
Priv.[20÷5] €13-18 c/Azabachería,15 © 981 071 254. **14●** **Mundoalbergue** *Priv.*
[34÷1] €12-€17 c/San Clemente, 26 © 981 588 625. **15●** **Roots & Boots** *Priv.*
[48÷8] €12-18 r/Campo Cruceiro do Galo © 699 631 594. **16●** **La Estación** *Priv.*
[24÷2] €12 r/Xoana Nogueira, 14 © 981 594 624 (½ km *far* side of railway station).

❏ *Hoteles:* ■ *€30 – €60:* *Hs* **Moure** © 981 583 637 r/dos Loureiros. *Hs* **Moure-II**
r/Laureles 12. *H* **Fonte de San Roque** © 981 554 447 r/do Hospitalillo, 8. *Hs* **La**
Campana © 981 584 850 Campanas de San Juan, 4. *Hs* **Estrela** © 981 576 924
Plaza de San Martín Pinario, 5-2° *Hospedería* **San Martín Pinario** © 981 560 282
Praza da Inmaculada. **Pico Sacro** r/San Francisco, 22 y **Pico Sacro II** © 981 584
466. **La Estela** © 981 582 796 rua Raxoi, 1. *Hs* **Barbantes** © 981581 077 r/do
Franco, 3. **Santa Cruz** © 981 582 362 r/do Vilar, 42. *Hs* **Suso** © 981 586 611 r/do
Vilar, 65. **San Jaime** © 981 583 134 r/do Vilar, 12-2°. **A Nosa Casa** © 981 585 926
r/Entremuralles, 9. *Hs* **Mapoula** © 981 580 124 r/Entremuralles, 10. *Hs* **Alameda**
© 981 588 100 San Clemente, 32 ■ *€60+:* *H* **Rua Vilar** © 981 557 102 r/Vilar,
12-2° *H* **Airas Nunes** © 902 405 858 r/do Vilar, 17. **Entrecercas** © 981 571 151 r/
Entrecercas. **Costa Vella** © 981 569 530 Porta de Pena, 17. **MV Algalia** © 981 558
111 Praziña da Algalia de Arriba, 5. ■ *€100+: H**** **San Francisco** Campillo de San
Francisco ©981 581 634. *H******Hostal de los Reyes Católicos** Plaza Obradoiro ©
981 582 200

❏ *Centro Histórico*: ❶ Convento de Santo Domingo de Bonaval XIIIth *(panteón*
de Castelao, Rosalía de Castro y museo do Pobo Galego). ❷ Casa Gótica XIVth
museo das Peregrinaciónes-1. ❸ Mosteiro de San Martín Pinario XVIth *y museo* ■
Prazo Obradoiro ❹ Pazo de Xelmirez XIIth ❺ Catedral XIIth –XVIIIth *Portica de*
Gloria, claustro, museo e tesouro da catedral ❻ Hostal dos Reis Católicos XVth
Parador ❼ Pazo de Raxoi XVIIIth *Presendencia da Xunta* ❽ Colexio de Fonseca
XVIth *universidade y claustro.* ❾ Casa do Deán XVIIIth *Oficina do Peregrino.* **10●**
Casa Canónica *museo Peregrinaciónes-2.* **11●** Mosteiro de San Paio de Anteltares
XVth *Museo de Arte Sacra.* **12●** S.Maria Salomé XIIth.

Santiago is a wonderful destination, full of vibrancy and colour. Pilgrims, street artists, musicians, dancers, tourists... all come and add to the life and soul of this fabled city. Stay awhile and visit her museums and markets. Soak up some of her culture or relax in the delightful shaded park *Alameda* and climb to the *capela de Santa Susanna* hidden in the trees or stroll up the Avenue of the Lions *Paseo dos Leónes* to the statue of Rosalia de Castro and look out west over her belovéd Galicia and... *Finis terre.*

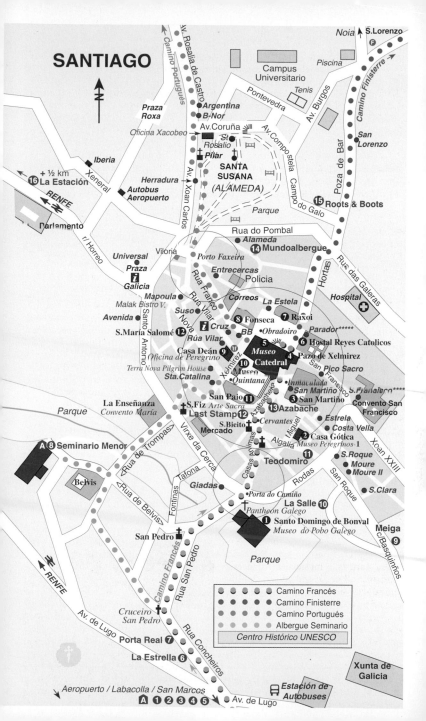

❒ **We walk by faith, not by sight.** *Corinthians 5:7*

1 SANTIAGO – NEGREIRA – 21.2 km

⁓⁓⁓⁓⁓⁓	--- ---	6.8	--- ---	32%
▬▬▬	--- ---	13.4	--- ---	63%
▬▬▬	--- ---	1.0	--- ---	0.5%
Total km		**21.2** km (13.2 ml)		

23.8 km (+^ 525m = 2.6 km)
Alto ▲ Trasmonte 285m (935 ft)
<Ⓐ Ⓗ> Lombao **10.5** km *Castelo (+500m)* – Chancela **20.5** *Logrosa (+700m)*.

❒ **The Practical Path:** This is the shortest and least strenuous stage. Recent work by the *Amigos* has increased natural pathways to 32% much of it through eucalyptus and pine forest which offers shade from the sun or shelter from the rain. Be prepared for the long climb (2.8 km) from Augapesada up to Trasmonte. Stay alert for old waymarks that direct you back onto the roads such as the busy C-543. Waymarking is not as clear as on the *Camino Francés* from Sarria and there will be 90% less pilgrims to help with directions! Drinking fonts are few and far between so fill up before leaving Santiago.

❒ **The Mystical Path:** We are surrounded by trivia. There is much to distract us from the inner path, but what profit is there in the outward journey if it is not accompanied by expanded awareness? A pilgrim must travel on two paths simultaneously. The tourist will look for the stone altar, the pilgrim an altered state. The one seeks sacred sites the other in-sight. Will we make time today for contemplation and reflection?

❒ **The Bible in Spain:** "... I have always found in the disposition of the children of the fields a more determined tendency to religion and piety than amongst the inhabitants of the towns and cities, and the reason is obvious – they are less acquainted with the works of man's hands than those of God... the scoffers at religion do not spring from amongst the simple children of nature, but are the excrescences of over-wrought refinement." *George Borrow*

❒ **Personal Notes:** "... *From this elevated hamlet I take a last backward glance to the cathedral spires and notice a sex-worker and her dishevelled client in the process of completing their transaction and reflect on the incongruous nature of city life and the confused borders between sexuality and spirituality – the sacred and the profane all bound up in the human story of Sodom and Gomorrah. I turn my back on the city, glad to be heading into the simplicity of the countryside.*"

0.0 km **Leave the cathedral** by the main (west) entrance and take the access road down between the Parador car park and police station past Igrexa de San Fructuoso. Proceed along the rúa das Hortas and cross over the busy intersection (❖*Farmacia*

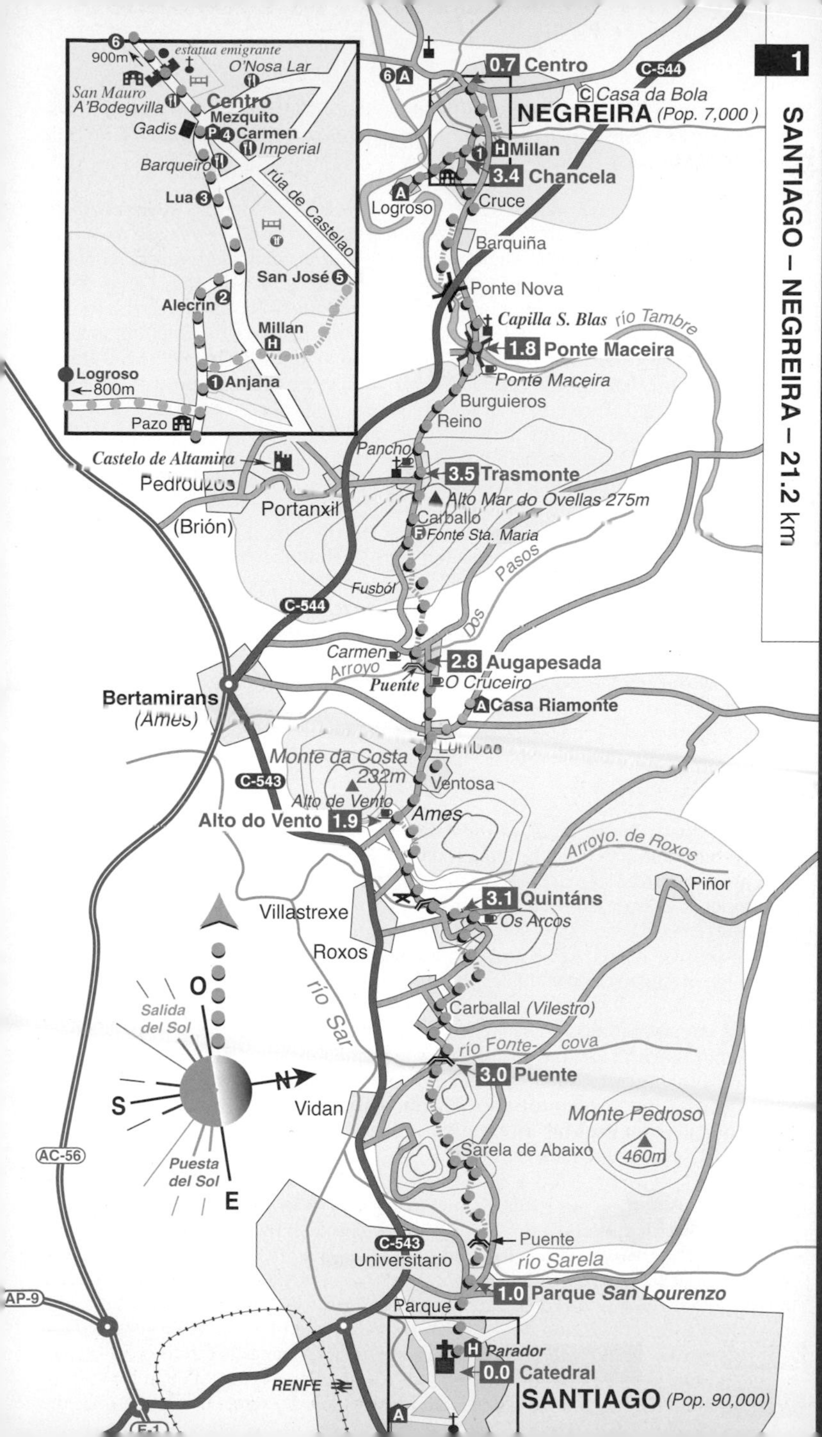

NEGREIRA (Pop. 7,000)

C-544

ⓒ Casa da Bola

0.7 Centro

Ⓗ Millan

3.4 Chancela

Cruce

Logroso

Ⓐ

Barquiña

Ponte Nova

✝ Capilla S. Blas   rio Tambre

1.8 Ponte Maceira

Ponte Maceira

Burguieros

Reino

Pancho

3.5 Trasmonte

▲ Alto Mar do Ovellas 275m

Carballo

✝ Fonte Sta. Maria

Fusból

Dos Pasos

Carmen

Arroyo

Puente

2.8 Augapesada

O Cruceiro

Ⓐ Casa Riamonte

Lombas

Ventosa

Monte da Costa 232m ▲

Alto de Vento

Ames

Alto do Vento **1.9**

Arroyo. de Roxos

Piñor

Villastrexe

3.1 Quintáns

Roxos

Os Arcos

Carballal (Vilestro)

rio Fonte- cova

3.0 Puente

Monte Pedroso

Sarela de Abaixo

▲ 460m

río Sar

Vidan

AC-56

Salida del Sol

O

S   N

Puesta del Sol

E

AP-9

C-543

Universitario

← Puente
río Sarela

1.0 Parque San Lourenzo

Parque

RENFE

E-1

✝ Ⓗ Parador

0.0 Catedral

SANTIAGO (Pop. 90,000)

Ⓐ

Bertamirans
(Ames)

C-543

C-544

Pedrouzos
(Brión)

Castelo de Altamira

Portanxil

Inset map (top left)

❻ 900m

estatua emigrante

O'Nosa Lar

San Mauro
A'Bodegvilla

Centro

Mezquito

Gadis

Ⓟ ❹ Carmen

Barqueiro

Ⓔ Imperial

Lua ❸

rúa de Castelao

Ⓜ

San José ❺

Alecrin ❷

Millan
Ⓗ

Logroso
←800m

Anjana ❶

Pazo

❻Ⓐ

right) at **Campo das Hortas [0.4** km] into rúa Poza do Bar (Alb. Roots and Boots left) passing *H***San Lorenzo** to park of ancient oak trees at **Carballeira de San Lorenzo [0.6** km]

1.0 km **Parque** *San Lorenzo* Adj. the park is Convento de San Lorenzo de Trasouto *XIII. [An alternative route from the Cathedral via the Parque de Santa Susanna joins from the left].* The small park offers shaded seating and fountain. We now have a tranquil 3 km of path through woodland. Waymarks take us down a steep concrete road to a stone bridge over the **río Sarela [0.4** km] veer <left over the river onto path alongside derelict mill across small stream to climb up through mixed woodland where the path rejoins a quiet road in the small hamlet of **Sarela de Abaixo [0.7** km] Here we can take a last look back to the spires of the cathedral and the city of Santiago. Turn down <left past the row of new houses and turn up right> **(past Nº 53) [0.2** km] and take path through the Eucalyptus forest on a rough walled lane to the top of a rise. The path now descends to rejoin asphalt road and down to bridge over the **rio Fontecova [1.7** km]

3.0 km **Puente** *rio Fontecova (tributary of the rIo Sar)*. S/o up steeply veering right> to T-junction and turn down <left into **Carballal** (parish of Vilestro) veer right> by bus-stop at village signboard and horreo. Continue out of the village and down to cross small stream and turn up steeply right> by high orchard wall onto woodland path crossing several local roads and up to village crossroads at:

3.1 km **Quintáns** *Bar Os Arcos (right)* turn <left and imm. right> by bus shelter down steeply turning right> at T-junction to **Puente rio Roxos [0.6** km] with picnic tables in shaded glade adj. the bridge over the river. The road takes us through **Portela** where the path then turns right> into woodland to emerge onto the **main road [1.3** km] at:

1.9 km **Alto de Vento** popular *Café* **Alto do Vento**. Here we pass into the Concello de Ames and continue down the main road AC-453 veering right> through the village of **Ventosa** and over [!] main road onto track and back to main road up to crossroads at **Lombao [1.5** km]. *[short detour 500m off route (right) alb.* **Casa Riamonte** *Priv. [6÷1]+* €12 (+€50-60) © 981 890 356 *(dinner available with Julián].* Continue s/o passing *Café* **O Cruceiro [0.8** km] and adj. ✤*Farmacia* turning <left to the medieval footbridge in Augapesada and back up to road **[0.5** km]:

2.8 km **Augapesada** continue s/o over road onto concrete path. *Bar/shop* Carmen *(50m left).* From here it's a steep uphill climb for 2.8 km through pine and eucalyptus forest. The track emerges onto the main road by radio mast. Continue past wayside fountain and picnic area **fonte Santa Maria Trasmonte** shortly afterwards we reach the high point **Alto do Mar de Ovellas** at 285m and then down through the small hamlet of **Carballo** and into **Trasmonte.**

3.5 km **Trasmonte** crossroads hamlet with *Bar* **Casa Pancho**. Cruceiro of St. James and Parish church of Santa Maria with baroque tower just off route on the road to the left. *Detour: This is also the road to the ruins of the Castelo de Altamira. A 4 km round trip by road via Portanxil, Leboráns to A Torre above Brións – **not** waymarked see map front cover).* From Trasmonte it's all the way downhill through the small hamlets of: **Reino** *(note sign left for mesón O Pozo 80m is in fact 300m down steeply on main road!).* **Burgueiros** and finally Ponte Maceira.

1.8 km **Ponte Maceira** riverside *Restaurante* overlooking the weir and the magnificent medieval bridge (restored) that crosses over wide río Tambre. This makes a delightful place to rest and, perhaps, bathe the feet in the cool waters. The hamlet is one of the best-preserved in Galicia with fine mansions *pazos* lining the river bank and houses with armorial shields. In a legend, reminiscent of the Red Sea biblical story, we are told that God destroyed the bridge in a single stroke to prevent Roman soldiers based at Dugium (Duio in Fisterra) pursuing the followers of St. James. This enduring myth lives on in the coat of arms of the local council. A reflection, perhaps, of the continuing split between the authority of church and state and between inner and outer authority. As Ralph Waldo Emerson reminds us in *Essays of the Over-Soul*, 'The faith that stands on authority is not faith.'

Ponte Maceira

Concello de Negreira

Once over the river you enter the ***Concello de Negreira***. Turn <left over the bridge passing the Capilla de San Blas and wayside cross *cruceiro* (left) and fonte (right). Veer <left onto track through oak woods alongside river under arch of the road bridge *Puente Nuevo*. The path meanders through crop fields to rejoin the road by car showrooms in Outeiros. Continue through Barca and turn up <left at next junction (signposted A Chancela / Logrosa) past 14thC Pazo Albariña (left).

Here legend tells of the lord of this Manor House who left his son in the care of a nurse while he went on a crusade against the Moors. When he returned he learnt that his son had drowned in the waters of the Río Tambre. He demanded the nurse be beheaded and at the moment the axe fell her husband also knelt with her and both were decapitated together. They were buried amongst the pines trees and it is said that the sighing of the pines here reflects their last embrace. This story is also reminiscent of the theme in the Galician anthem The Pines Os Pinos that calls on Galicians to listen to the murmuring pines which is none other than the voice of the ancestors calling on the people to throw off the yoke of oppression and servitude.

`3.4 km` **Chancela de Abaixo** *Options* Here we find the first (and newest) of the pilgrim hostels spread out through Negreira *(Note: the municipal hostel is still 1.6 km the far side of the town centre)*. Alb.❶ **Anjana** *Priv.[18÷3]* €12 with bar and terrace © 667 204 706 (Sara y Miguel) Lugar de la Chancela, 39. Here we also have:

Option [1]: Logrosa Detour 0.8 km: ● ● ● ● *Alb.* **Logrosa** *Priv.[20÷2]*+ €17incl. (+€30-50 priv.) © 981 885 820 (m: 646 142 554 Antonio y Luis). Direction: *Turn down opp. Anjana and continue for 800m past church (left) into Logrosa to the albergue (signposted right). Welcoming hostel and quiet garden. Dinner available and, maybe, Queimada/Conxuro traditional Galician ritual drink.*
Option [2]: Take lane (right) imm. after Anjana to go direct to *H*****Millan** (prev. Tamara) €30-45 © 981 885 201 Av. Santiago. Behind the hotel is short-cut through woodland to *alb.* ❺ **San José** *Priv.[50÷3]*+ €12 (+ €20-45) © 881 976 934 (Débora y Victoria) on rúa de Castelao 400m from the town centre.

Continue s/o to rejoin main road into Negreira. Here is a pilgrim information kiosk and 50m (right) *Alb.* ❷ **Alecrin** *Priv.[40÷2]* €10 © 981 818 286 (Benigno Tuñas) Av. Santiago,52 (Hotel Millan beyond). For the town centre turn <left over rio de Duomes (tributary of río Tambre). Proceed up Av. de Santiago up past the modern statues of a medieval pilgrim and *Alb.* ❸ **Lua** *Priv.[40÷1]* €9 © 698 128 883 (Marcus y Pilar) Av. Santiago,22 modern building (left). Opposite Lua is secondary road to albergue San José.

0.7 km Negreira *Centro* central crossroads with *Gadis* supermarket (left) and *alb.* ❹ **Carmen** *Priv.[34÷2]*+ €10 (+ind.€30-50) © 636 129 691 (Mari Carmen) on calle del Carmen, 2 part of *Hostal y Restaurante* **La Mezquito**. The Municipal / Xunta albergue is located 900m out of town (see town plan). *alb.* ❺ **Municipal** *Xunta. [20÷2]* €6 © 664 081 498 (Charo y Paula) additional mattresses on the floor with good shower & toilet facilities and kitchenette (buy food before arriving) see photo right. Directions: (see way out stage 2).

Negreira with a population of 7,000 has a variety of shops, bank ATM's and the local council office *Concello de Negreira* © 981 885 550 and taxi rank © 981 885 515 / also Taxi Ramón © 626 033 879 centrally located off calle Carmen. There are several bars and restaurants incl. the popular Imperial © 981 885 579 c/Carmen with terrace to the rear where Pilar and English husband David provide home cooking from 12:00 onwards or try the central Barqueiro on Av. Santiago. Cervecería Galaecia on c/San Mauro serves breakfast from 6:30 a.m. and further down the

street is A'Bodegvilla popular with pilgrims requiring snack food (12:00 to 22:00 see photo right). 1.5 km out of town off the AC-546 is *CR* **Casa de Bola** (Michelin guide) from €65 © 670 648 078. The towns relative modernity belies its early foundations. The coat of arms of the local council portray the destruction of the bridge over the Río Tambre, thus saving St. James' disciples from pursuit and securing the legend of Santiago (see photos previous page).

The illustrious Counts of Altamira, whose power in the 15th century extended over the whole of this area to the walls of Santiago city itself, occupied the manor house and chapel of Saint Mauro that we pass at the start of stage 2. Their main seat was Castelo Altamira now in ruins (located off the camino 2 km from Trasmonte - see front cover). Just below the arch is a delightful shaded square with benches and fountain and here we find a masterpiece in evocative sculpture of an émigré leaving his family to seek work in the brave New World. It reflects the constant emigration, particularly of men, from Galicia down through the ages.

Note: The next stage is the longest at 34.0 kilometres and you will need to start early if you intend to reach Olveiroa by evening. However several new albergues provide intermediate lodging and there is a free pick-up & drop-off service next day from As Maroñas / Santa Mariña to the following *off* route hotels: *A Picota* (+2.5 km) – Santa Baia (+11 km) – *Santa Comba* (+12 km) and Outes (+14 km)

REFLECTIONS:

❒ **As a well-spent day brings happy sleep, so life well used brings happy death.**
Leonardo da Vinci

2 NEGREIRA – OLVEIROA

▓▓▓▓▓▓▓	--- ---	11.0 --- ---	*33%*
▬▬▬	--- ---	22.3 --- ---	*66%*
▬▬▬	--- ---	<u>0.5</u> --- ---	*1%*
Total km		**33.8** km (21.0 ml)	

36.9 km (+^ 625m = 3.1 km)

Alto ▲ Monte Aro 420m (1,380 ft)

< Ⓐ Ⓗ > Vilaserío **13.0** km – Maroñas /S.Mariña **21.0** km – Abeleiros *A Picota* **28.4** *(+2.9)* – Mallon / Ponte Olveira **31.7** km

```
500m ------------------- Alto 440m ------------ Monte Aro 495m ▲ ● Castro --------
                                                        Castro ● ② ▲ 420m
400m ---- Portocamiño ▲Piaxe Vilaserío ---- Sta.Mariña ---------- S.Cristovo ----
         Rapoté Ⓕ              Ⓐ Ⓐ         Ⓗ Ⓐ                    ↑OLVEIROA
300m Zas ▥▥                              río Maroñas  ▥Maroñas        Mallón Ⓐ▥  Ⓐ
200m ▮S.Xulián                                                          río Xallas
Ⓐ
NEGREIRA                                      ┊21 km
0 km        5 km       10 km      15 km      20 km      25 km      30 km
```

❒ **The Practical Path:** This is a *very* long stage with 67% on hard road. However, there is now interim lodging esp. around Maroñas / Santa Mariña at 21.0 km which allows a shorter stage to Cee 19.0 km and an additional day to Finisterre (lighthouse) 15.6 km necessitating 4 days in total. Two hotels and a casa rural provide a pick-up service from Maroñas which alleviates pressure on lodging but this remains limited and flexibility may be required. Bring some energy snacks and full water bottles.

❒ **The Mystical Path:** We generally experience death and dying as unwelcome visitors. Yet to be born anew we must first allow our old out-worn perceptions die. Over-identification with our physical bodies limits our understanding of Who we are and induces fear and a sense of vulnerability. We need to let go of many old and cherished beliefs if we want to become part of the New.

❒ **Personal Notes:** *"... with what little strength remained I hung my soaking clothes across the open fire and raked the dying embers. As I stumbled up the stairs my candle blew out with the gale-force wind that howled through the broken window. I relit it and in the brief moment before it was again extinguished I caught the surreal reflection of numerous dolls scattered over the floor. I was aware that I was alone but the fear of loneliness died in me that night. Exhaustion flooded over me and sweet sleep came to drown out the noise of the storm outside..."*

0.0 km **Leaving the centre of Negreira** *[Albergue Carmen Mezquito crossroads]* head down calle San Mauro under the stone archway (emigrant statue right) s/o over **Río Barcala** veering <left at fork to sign for Negreira **Iglesia [0.7 km]** *[alb.* ❻ **Municipal** *Xunta s/o 200m]*. Turn off right> and head up past church of *San Xulián XVI* up steps onto laneway veering <left onto woodland path. Continue s/o up Alto da Cruz to rejoin the asphalt road into **Zas [2.3 km]**:

3.0 km **Zas** Turn right> by bus-stop and small shop (often closed) through Zas San Marmede onto woodland that winds its way up through eucalyptus and oak woods

rio Xallas

Fonte y Ermita Sta. Lucia 1.1

As Pías → C
Iglesia Santiago → 2.1 **Albergue**Xunta
Casa Loncho **Horreo** C 1
Casa Garrido → C **OLVEIROA**
(Pop. 200)   Olveira   Baiñas
Dolmen

A **O Refuxio**

Ponte Olveira 3.3   A **Ponte Olveira**
Mallon
*Embalse
da
Fervenza*

San Cristóvo †   Corzón

0.6 cruce
<0.5 camino
1.1> asfalto

A PICOTA   ←3.9 **Abeleiroas**
① *Casa Jurjo* H
(from Abeleiroas) 2.9   **minas**   Lago
0.8> camino   *Castro*   Monte Aro 555m
0.3> camino
Cruce (alto) 1.3^

2.9 **Castro-Opción**
Vilar do Castro   Gueima
† **Bon Xesús**

Cee 28.4 km

Negreira 24.5 km

LC-403

PINO DO VAL

*Dolmen
Perxubeira* 1.9   **Antelo**
A 0.6 **S.Mariña**
Casa Pepa
03a **Cee 31.9 km**
← **S.Mariña** 1.4 A
Chacin   **MAROÑAS**
(S.Baia)   ② *Santa Eulalia*   *collect / recogida*   ① *Casa Jurjo*
Eirón   4.5 **Puente**   ② *Santa Eulalia*
③ *Perfeuto Maria*
*Montes   ④ *Hotel Xallas*
de Eirón*
▲   Barbeira
505m   LC-403
H Xallas +12 km >

< Outes   Pesadoira

< Outes
③ < CR Perfeuto Maria +14 km   **Cornado** 2.1

A Nosa Casa   A **Escuela** (basico)
Vilaserío 4.4   A
O'Rueiro
Marcelle

Lebreiro

Cruceiro da Piaxe
Portocamiño   † 1.7 **Piaxe**

3.9 **Rapote**

Camiño Real
Campelo   San Martiño

LC-444 *Santa Comba >*
Zas 3.0 →
Alto do Cruz
San Xulián †
Xunta ⑥ A

rio Tambre

NEGREIRA   0.0 — **Centro** — **S. Mariña 21.0 km** 02a

O
*Puesta
del Sol*
S   N
*Salida
del Sol*
E

for a delightful 3.9 kilometres of forest track that skirts around *Camiño Real* crossing a quiet road to San Martiño into:

3.9 km **Rapote** *[F.] Fuente da Rapote* The way continues through woodland s/o past turn-off back left **[1.4 km]** *[to main road at Portocamiño 200m off route with bar]* continue s/o past igrexa San Mamede da Pena into *Piaxe* **[0.3 km]**.

1.7 km **Piaxe** *A Pena* with wayside cruceiro. Continue up and turn right on main road [!] (*Portocamiño left*) past sign for *Parque Eólico de Corzón* (part of the extensive wind turbine infrastructure of Galicia) and veer s/o right at **junction [0.9 km]** onto earthen track (by sign for Lebreiro) which winds its way back to the **main road** [!] **[1.0 km]**. Stay on the CP-5603 and watch out for turn off **<left [2.1 km]** [!] ('70 kph' sign) onto path down to **Vilaserío [0.4 km]**.

4.4 km **Vilaserío** *Alb.* **O Rueiro** *Priv.[32÷3]* €12 ✆ 981 893 561 (Jesús Puñal) m: 659 568 139 adj. to the popular café/bar Herminio / A Nosa Casa. Continue on main road to old **schoolhouse [0.5 km]** *Alb.* **Escuela** *Muni.[14÷3]* € donation ✆ 648 792 029 (key with Nidia who lives in No 39 blue facade opp). Very basic hostel (undergoing repairs in 2015) with 10 mattresses *colchonetas* on ground floor + 3 rooms upstairs . Continue on main road to turn-off right> into **Cornado [1.6 km]**:

2.1 km **Cornado** *[F.] Fuente de Cornada* and turn up <left onto another forest track right> on main road and <left back onto farm tracks into **Maroñas [4.5 km]**:

4.5 km **As Maroñas** *Puente* s/o over bridge *río Maroñas* (good picnic spot) and into *Concello de Mazaricos*. Turn <left at crossroads and <left again at T-Junction [Note: right As Maroñas with panadería on main road and pick-up for hotel Xallas].

1.4 km **Santa Mariña** *As Maroñas* wayside cross – 50m left for *Alb.***Casa Pepa** *Priv.[16÷1]+* €12 ✆ 981 852 881 (Flora y Paco) with popular bar (see photo right). *Note:* if hostels in Santa Mariña are full or there is no time or energy to reach Olveiroa phone the following *off* route hotels who offer a free pick-up and drop-off service the following morning to pilgrims as follows:

❶ *H* **Casa Jurjo** €40-60 ✆ 981 852 015 *A Picota* +2.9 km (also accessible on foot)
❷ *H* **Santa Eulalia** €40+ ✆ 981 877 262 *Santa Baia* +11 km
❸ *H* **Xallas** €35-60 ✆ 981 880 708 *Santa Comba* +12 km
❹ *CR* **Casa Perfeuto Maria** €54 full board (min.2) ✆ 981 851 009 *Outes* +14 km

To continue turn right at wayside cross past picnic area (left) and <left on main road (LC-403) passing *Café/bar* Casa Vitoriano to *bar Gallego /* Antelo and adjoining:

0.6 km **Santa Mariña** *LC-403* *Alb.* **Antelo** *Priv.[10÷2]* €10 ✆ 981 852 897 m: 655 806 800 renovated stone building on the main road and alternative pick-up point *recogida* for off route hotels.

From Bar Antelo /albergue continue to turn off **right>** [**0.3** km] (signposted Bon Xesus) onto minor road with Monte Aro now visible ahead. Pass wayside cross through the hamlets of **Bon Xesus** [**1.5** km] (site of a medieval pilgrim hospital) and **Xeima** and up to a camino **signboard** [**1.1** km].

2.9 km   Castro *Signboard Option* [!] The original track via the north side of Monte Aro is now closed and a provisional route is waymarked around the base of the hill (right) on a quiet asphalt road. An alternative route south of the summit (through the line of windmills on the crest) is shown in green on the map. It is poorly waymarked with green dots (tennis ball size). It is the same distance but with a steep climb up Monte Aro at the start but all the way down is by delightful woodland pathways. It rejoins the road route just before Corzón as follows:

● ● ● ● *Alternative Route via Monte Aro – 6.0 km.* Turn <left at signboard and up right> [**0.3** km] by high concrete wall and follow the road up to the top and s/o over crossroads [**1.0** km] 495m *(Celtic castro up right 800m with 360° views from the summit at 550m)*. Continue through the line of windmills (see photo below) and take the track right> [**0.3** km] into woodland and fork right> *[!]* [**0.8** km] passing abandoned mine [**0.3** km] and turn right> on road [**0.8** km] *(Note: A Picota 1.6 km left at this point)* and <left off road [**0.5** km] to rejoin the waymarked route [**0.6** km]. We now turn <left and immediately right> to follow the road into Corzón [**1.3** km].

Detour [1] ● ● ● ● *A Picota – 2.9 km*: At the bus shelter in Abeleiroas (alt. free pick-up point for **Casa Jurjo.**) it is only 2.9 km into *A Picota* This is a useful option in the high season when accommodation in the area is sometimes full. To walk this detour follow the quiet country road (left), ignoring any turn-offs, directly into A Picota. If you are walking the alternative route (above) via Monte Aro then turn <left when you reach the main road and *A Picota* is only 1.6 km from this point.

Detour [2] ● ● ● ● *Dolmen Perxubeira – 1.9 km.* Erected 4000 years ago as a site of sacred ritual and worship. It is easily accessed but little visited. Directions: From albergue Antelo continue on the main road in direction of Muros/Pino do Val *past* the turn-off (right) for Bon Xesus and Forxas/ Abaxio to junction (left) for Corbeira/Eirón. The dolmen is 200m down a track to the side of the large two-storey house on the corner. It is located in a field (private land – show due care and respect) on the far side of the young plantation. Return the same way. (Casa Jurjo can arrange a visit by taxi).

For the waymarked provisional road route turn right> by sign and follow the waymarks along the quiet country lanes with distant views of the reservoir *Embalse da Fervenza*. Turn <**left [0.8** km] and <left again **[1.7** km] onto farm track into **Lago** back to the road in **Portaliñas [1.0** km] (seating) and into **Abeleiroas [0.4** km].

3.9 km   Abeleiroas bus-stop *[2.9 km to A Picota (left) or phone Casa Jurjo. Note: this is the closest ½ way lodging between Negreira (28.4 km) and Cee (24.5 km)].* Taxi Mazaricos ✆ 608 292 018. Continue right> past *alternative 'green route' via Monte Aro track* (left) **[0.7** km] all the way by old (worn) asphalt road into **Corzón [1.4** km] Igrexa de San Cristóbal. *[plans to renovate the ruins of the casa rectoral as an albergue have stalled. Over to the right are the Montes de la Ruña and the highest peak Monte do Castelo/ Ruña (645m) is the site of a medieval castle with legends of buried gold!].* Pass the cemetery and turn <left to cross the *rio Mazariscos* and water mill *Muiño de Mallón* (left). Turn right> in the village of **Mallon [1.2** km].

3.3 km   Ponte Olveira / Mallón on corner of main road is the recently restored (2015) traditional town house now converted to an albergue. *Alb.* ❶ **Ponte Olveira** *Priv.[20÷1]*+ €12 + priv. €30-40 ✆ 981 852 135 (Alba) m: 603 450 145. Continue s/o over the **río Xallas** *Concello de Dumbria*

to *Alb.*❷ **O Refuxio** *Priv.[10÷1]* €10 ✆ 981 741 724 (José Manuel) m: 655 620 180. Continue along main road and shortly after passing the sign (right) for Olveira (*not* OlveirOa) pass *hostal* **Casa Garrido** B&B from €15 ✆ 674 260 638 *(also own O Peregrino in Olveiroa)* and take the slip road <left into Olveiroa centre:

2.1 km   Olveiroa *Alb.* ❶ **Hórreo** *Priv. [53÷5]*+ €12 ✆ 981 741 673 m: 617 026 005 part of the adj. *CR* **Casa Loncho** with private rooms from €40 All facilities incl. restaurant, laundry, taxi. *Alb.* ❷ **Olveiroa** *Xunta.[46÷5]* €6 ✆ 658 045 242 (Puri) one of the more inspiring Xunta hostels, reconstructed from traditional houses on either side of a quiet village lane. Adj. *café/ bar* O Peregrino *(see casa Garrido).* Finally

*Pr********As Pías** €40-60 ✆ 981 741 520 m: 617 026 005 handsomely reconstructed traditional stone house with restaurant/bar and terrace that gets the evening sun.

The village 'square' has a collection of interesting hórreos and just beyond is the parochial church **Igrexa Santiago** *XII* with statue of Saint James above the west door. A short detour (1 km) off the main road is the tiny hermitage of Santa Lucía adjoining the river and fountain of the same name. *[Here an endearing tradition is to heal eye ailments by washing them in the clear spring waters and dry them on a handkerchief, which is then also left out to dry – an allusion to drying the tears of remorse at past wrongs in order to heal spiritual blindness and refresh psyche and soul].* Taxi service between hostels and tourist sites in the area such as the waterfall at Ézaro; available from Taxi Loncho (Olveiroa) ✆ 981 741 673 m: 617 026 005 also Antonio at Taxi Mazaricos (A Picota) m: 608 292 018.

REFLECTIONS:

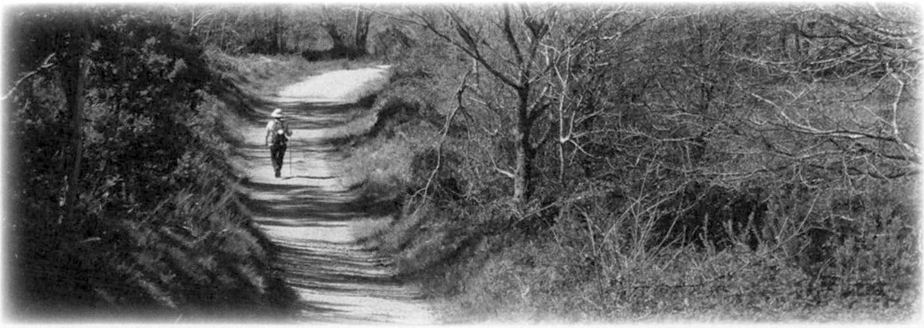

◻ **Faith is the substance of things hoped for
The evidence of things not seen.** *Hebrews 11.1*

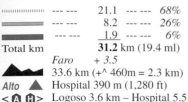

---

3 OLVEIROA – FINISTERRE *centro*

⊪⊪⊪⊪⊪⊪	--- ---	21.1	--- ---	68%
▬▬▬	--- ---	8.2	--- ---	26%
▬▬▬	--- ---	1.9	--- ---	6%
Total km		**31.2** km (19.4 ml)		

Faro + 3.5
33.6 km (+^ 460m = 2.3 km)

Alto ▲ Hospital 390 m (1,280 ft)

< Ⓐ Ⓗ > Logoso 3.6 km – Hospital 5.5 km – Cee 18.2 km – Corcubión 19.8
San Roque 22.1 – Estorde 24.2 km – Sardiñiero 25.2 km.

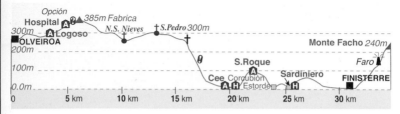

◻ **The Practical Path:** Another long day but if tiredness overtakes lodging is available in Cee (or Dumbria on the alternative route). The route splits in Hospital with the option to go directly to Finisterre or Muxía. *[Note: if you intend to go direct to Muxía see maps on pages 110-112 for this counter-clockwise route].* 70% of the route to Finisterre is on natural pathways including one of the most isolated stages on the whole camino with no facilities whatsoever on this stretch of 12.3 km.

◻ **The Mystical Path:** What purpose brought us this far? Without faith we are lost indeed. To walk through this life without a spiritual focus is to travel down a cul-de-sac called despair with only our own mortality waiting for us at the end. To walk the inner camino with a pure motive and openness of mind is to journey to the source of our own immortality. Will we take time today to reflect on the purpose of our life and the means of fulfilling it? The final lesson for each soul is the total surrender to the Will of God manifested in our own hearts.

◻ **Personal Notes:** "… too exhausted to undo the straps on my backpack I collapsed at the side of the road. The last thing I remembered was the rain falling on my face, my lower back locked in spasm. I don't know how long I remained there but when I came round the spasm had miraculously gone. I was lying at the foot of a medieval cross with a figure of Christ crucified looking down at me. It was strange I had not noticed it before…

… it was late in the day, as I came down the hill from the Ara Solis, when a luminescent light appeared out of the gloom. It had rained incessantly for 10 days and now on the last day the sun was beginning to break through. I became aware of a butterfly hovering above the path and the tears started to fall – I had emerged from my own chrysalis and in that moment knew it was not the outer journey but the inner focus that would be the new basis for my life. I write these notes from a balcony looking east over Monte Pindo. A Course In Miracles lies open to remind me that, *All my past, except its beauty, is gone and nothing is left but a blessing.*"

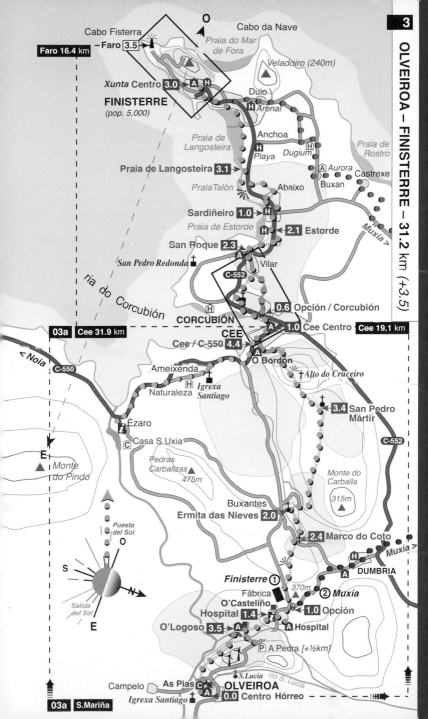

O

Cabo da Nave

Cabo Fisterra
–**Faro** 3.5

Faro 16.4 km

Praia do Mar de Fora

Veladoiro (240m)

Xunta Centro 3.0 A H

FINISTERRE
(pop. 5,000)

Duio

H *Arenal*

Anchoa

H
Praia de Langosteira
Playa

Dugium

Praia de Rostro

Praia de Langosteira 3.1

A *Aurora*
Castrexe

PraiaTalón

Abaixo

Buxan

Sardiñeiro 1.0 H

Praia de Estorde

H 2.1 **Estorde**

San Roque 2.3 A

San Pedro Redonda †

Vilar

Muxía >

C-552

ria do Corcubión

0.6 **Opción / Corcubión**

H

CORCUBIÓN

A 1.0 **Cee Centro**   **Cee 19.1 km**

03a **Cee 31.9 km**

CEE

< Noia

Cee / C-550 4.4 A

C-550

Ameixenda

O Bordón

A

† *Alto do Cruceiro*

Naturaleza

H *Igrexa Santiago*

†

Ézaro

Casa S.Uxia

C

3.4 **San Pedro Mártir**

†

C-552

Monte do Pindo

E

Pedras Carballizas 475m

Monte do Carballa 315m

Buxantes

Ermita das Nieves 2.0

2.4 **Marco do Coto**

Puesta del Sol

O

S

N

Muxía >

H
A **DUMBRIA**

Finisterre ①

Fábrica

370m

② *Muxía*

O'Casteliño

1.0 **Opción**

Hospital 1.4

A **Hospital**

O'Logoso 3.5 A

P **A Pedra** [+½km]

Salida del Sol

E

† *S.Lucia*

rio S. Lucia

Campelo

As Pias C A

OLVEIROA

Igrexa Santiago †

0.0 **Centro Hórreo**

03a **S.Mariña**

`0.0 km` **Leaving Olveiroa albergue** pass *CR As Pias* turn <left over stream ***Rego do Santa Lucia*** onto secondary road and turn up right> to follow track onto open moorland with extensive views up the valley of the Río Xallas (left) which widens here to form a small reservoir *Embalse de Ponte Olveira y Castrelo*. Continue along track towards windfarm through young forest plantation and follow the contour line westwards over *rio do Hospital* and up into:

`3.5 km` **Logoso** hamlet with welcoming *cafe /Alb.* **Logoso** *Priv.[22÷3]*+ €12 -€30 ℃ 981 727 602 (Domingo) m: 659 505 399. *[Family also run Pensión A Pedra on main road ½ km off route].* Veer <left up to rejoin the main road in Hospital.

`1.4 km` **Hospital** pilgrim information *Centro de Información ao Peregrino de Hospital* (Dumbría) ℃ 981 744 001. The original village was raised to the ground by Napoleon's troops during the peninsular war. In the medieval period it supported a pilgrim hospital and since 2015 the village has a replacement! To head for the new hostel (300m *off* route) turn *down* main road and cross over into the village where the hostel is on located at the lower end *Alb.* ❶ **Hospital** *Priv.[22÷3]* €12 ℃ 981 747 387. Managed by Javier (son of Marina) at the nearby O Casteliño directly on the waymarked route **[0.4 km]** *up* the main road. *Café/ Alb.* ❷ **O Casteliño** *Priv.[12÷2]* €12 ℃ 981 747 387 where Marina provides a 'last chance saloon' before venturing onto the open moorland beyond. The popular café also serves the nearby factory and a small cabina to the rear provides a basic albergue. The camino follows a bend in the old road for to our high point at 370m **Alto [0.6 km]:**

`1.0 km` **Cruce/ Option** here the route splits – Due West (left) for Finisterre or s/o North for Muxía. A marker on the central reservation indicates Fisterra 28 km / Muxía 27 km (Finisterre *lighthouse* and Muxía *sanctuary* respectively – *not* the town centres). If you plan to visit both (each has its unique flavour and pilgrimage tradition) there are advantages in proceeding clockwise to Finisterre and then continuing to Muxía. This way around you [1] walk downhill over

the moors with the first dramatic views of the sea and Cabo Finisterre. [2] benefit from an equally beautiful entry into Muxía along the coast from Finisterre. [3] Muxía provides a quieter space *off* the main camino for rest and reflection before returning home by bus or taxi. If you are returning on foot as part of the camino 'circuit' note waymarking is in *both* directions so extra vigilance is required. Whichever route you take there are challenges... and rewards. ***Note***: If you decide to walk *anti*-clockwise go to map on page 120.

For Finisterre turn <left along the unsightly carbide factory whose chimneys spew smoke making it visible for miles around. Trucks laden with iron ore thunder up and down the road between here and the industrial port in Cee. Opp. the factory car-park we turn off **right> [0.6 km]** onto the ancient Royal Way *Camino Real* and leave the incongruous factory behind us to pass over these isolated moors for a mystical 12.3 km.

Nearby are prehistoric stone carvings *Pedra Longa* engraved 4,000 years ago and the megalithic monuments *mamoas* and dolmens dotted around this sacred landscape. All bear witness to the antiquity of this route that our pagan forebears walked centuries before the Christian era dawned. This is also one of the areas associated with the mythical Vakner, '*... a terrifying creature, man-like, of a malignant nature, that lives like a troglodyte in the deepest and densest parts of the forest.*' It is suggested this mythic creature was used by the early Church to discourage the practise of pagan rites here. The mythic figure was probably based on the sighting of wild boar or bear that may have roamed these high moors. To heighten the sense of foreboding we can add the following myth of the assembly of departed souls *Estadéa* that wander about here visiting those who are to join them - referred to as the Holy Company *Santa Compaña* by H.V. Morton in *A Stranger in Spain*:

> *When you are travelling at night in Galicia, you may in certain marshy places see flickering lights which dart here and there over the mournful landscape. You must now be very careful. It may be that you will find an invisible presence trying to place a lighted candle in your hand, and should you open your hand and accept it, you are lost... So it can happen that you may simply disappear from life and spend an eternity trying to get rid of your candle, haunting the moorlands and the waste places where the ghostly lights flicker, until at last you can lure some human being into the Holy Company of Souls and escape yourself!'*

This is the high point of today's stage and providing you escape the *Vakner* and the *Santa Compaña* you will have your first view of the sea (providing you are also spared the rain or hill fog that *does frequent* this high moor). The path now slopes gently downhill through scrubland, mostly gorse and heather with pockets of young forestry to **road [1.8** km]:

2.4 km   **Marco do Couto** here we cross over road with 18thC wayside cross and adj. medieval marker-stone with the initials *RC* (likely reference to the Royal Way to Finisterre *Real Camino*). The waymarked route now follows the contour line before dropping down <left to:

2.0 km   **Ermita Nosa Señora das Nieves** 18thC *Hermitage of Our Lady of the Snows* and site of an annual local pilgrimage *romería* each September to this remote chapel and Holy Spring by the ancient stone cross in the field immediately below. The waters are said to have healing properties, particularly effective for nursing mothers. From here we cross over the 'river of snows' *Riego do Nievas* and make our way uphill to traverse the hillside opposite and join the track from Marco do Couto (right) **[2.6** km] where we continue by the edge of mature woodland past abandoned farm buildings to **hermitage [0.8** km]:

3.4 km   **Ermita San Pedro Martír** *[F.] Fuente San Pedro Martír* hermitage with shelter, water font and picnic area. Not to be outdone by Our Lady of the Snows – Saint Peter the Martyr cures bodily aches and rheumatism with the simple expedient of placing the diseased part of the body in the waters of the holy spring. The route continues along the ridge of the hill to **Cruceiro do Armada**

[2.2 km] the original stone cross has gone but a substitute marks the spot (100m *off* route). From here we get the first views over the *rias* of Cee and Corcubion with Monte Facho and Cabo Finisterre on the distant horizon (see photo) partly obscured by the woodland plantation. Continue steeply [!] downhill on a rocky track that winds its way through the pinewoods to an asphalt road [1.7 km] turn <left down to T-junction [0.2 km] where (50m left *off* route) on the outskirts of **Os Camiños Chans (Cee)** is *Alb.*❶ **O Bordón** *Priv.[24÷1]* €12 ℂ 981 746 574 (Pedro) m: 655 903 932. To continue towards Cee turn right> at T-junction to pass wayside cross to the main road at **Os Camiños Chans [0.3 km].**

4.4 km   C-550 / Cee / Os Camiños Chans / *Option* Café Casa Talieiro.* This the industrial port of Cee with several **Options:** (see town map). To make it to Finisterre in the shortest possible time:
[1] Follow the waymarked route around the coast direct to **Finisterre.**
[2] Explore **Cee** town with a good choice of albergues, hotels and restaurants.
[3] Detour by road to **Ameixenda** Church (**2.8** km – see next page).
[4] Detour by road to **Ézaro** Waterfall (**11.4** km – see next page).

[1] To continue on the waymarked route towards Finisterre (bypassing Cee town centre) turn right> in **Camiños Chans** along the busy *Ruta Atlántica* C-550 pass the cemetery and veer off <left down towards the Paseo Maritimo:

1.0 km   Cee *Option* Alb.*❷ **Moreira** *Priv.[14÷2]*+ €12 +€25-30 ℂ 981 746 282 (José Manuel Moreira) m: 620 891 547 c/ Rosalia de Castro, 75 with fine views over the bay. To continue direct to Finisterre via Corcubión keep s/o down the steps to the Paseo y Parque Maritimo and town beach *Praia da Concha* with modern shopping centre and hospital on our right.

[2] To explore Cee or stay the night turn right> into rúa Magdalena *(Escolar Infantil)* pass *H******Larry** €35+ ℂ 981 746 441 rúa Madgdelena with popular basement restaurant (left) and ❶ *Pazo do Cotón y Cruceiro da Fonte Penín (drinking font at rear)* and *Alb.*❸ **A Casa da Fonte** *Priv.[42÷2]* €10 ℂ 981 746 663 (Guzmán) m: 699 242 711 Rúa de Arriba, 36. At this point there is a choice of camino waymarks **[a]** Turn down <left emerging in Praza da Constitución with ❷ *Iglesia de Nuestra Señora da Xunqueira* (see photo) in front

of this restored XV[th]C parish church is a monument to the town's famous architect Domingo de Andrade who also designed the clock tower in Santiago cathedral.
[b] To continue towards the town centre and additional lodging keep s/o merging back onto the C-550 and the Av. Fernando Blanco with *H** **La Marina** €45 ℂ 981 746 511 on busy junction in the centre. Waymarks continue to the Av. Finisterre and turn left to pass: *P****Casa Crego** ℂ 981 745 947 and the adj. *H*******Insua** €40+ ℂ 981 747 575 part of *Alb.* ❹ **Camino das Estrelas** *Priv.[30÷3]* €12-15. Just before entering Corcubión *P** **Beiramar** ℂ 981 745 040 m: 670 90 52 98 Av. Finisterre, 220 (also own *albergue* **Camiño Fisterra** see Corcubión).

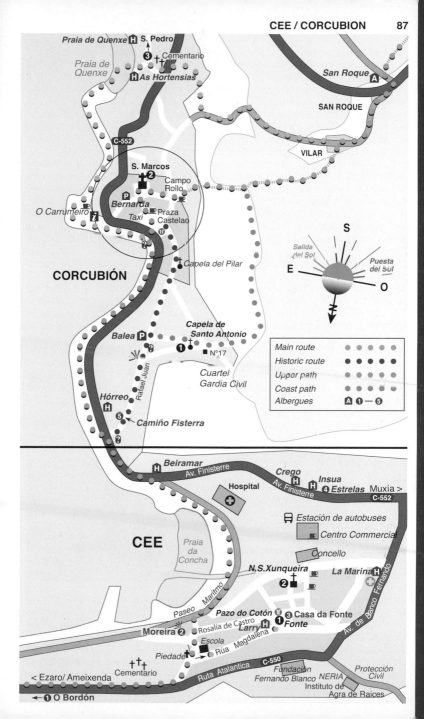

Praia de Quenxe 🏨 S. Pedro
❸ ✝ *Cementario*
Praia de Quenxe
🏨 **As Hortensias**

San Roque Ⓐ

SAN ROQUE

C-552

VILAR

S. Marcos
✝❷ Campo Rollo
🅿
Bernarda
O Carrumeiro
7
Taxi ✝ *Praza Castelao*

CORCUBIÓN

✝ *Capela del Pilar*

S
Salida del Sol
E
O
Puesta del Sol

Capela de Santo Antonio
Balea 🅿
❶ ✝
Nº17
Cuartel Gardia Civil

Main route ● ● ●
Historic route ● ● ●
Upper path ● ● ●
Coast path ● ● ●
Albergues Ⓐ ❶ — ❺

Rafael Juan

Hórreo 🏨
5 ←
Camiño Fisterra

🏨 **Beiramar** Av. Finisterre
Crego 🏨
Insua
🏨 ❹ **Estrelas** Muxía >
Av. Finisterre
C-552

Hospital ✚

🚏 *Estación de autobuses*
Centro Commercial

CEE
Praia da Concha
Concello

N.S.Xunqueira
❷ ✝
La Marina 🏨
✚

Paseo Marítimo

Pazo do Cotón ❸ **Casa da Fonte**
Moreira ❷ *Rosalía de Castro* **Larry** 🏨 ❶
Fonte
Escola *Rúa Magdalena*
Piedade ✝✝✝ *Cementario*
< Ezaro/ Ameixenda
← ❶ O Bordón
Ruta Atalantica C-550
Fundación Fernando Blanco NERIA
Protección Civil
Instituto de Agra de Raices
Av. de Banco Fernando

[2] Cee: A bustling commercial town serving the local fishing and industrial port and a resident population of 7,500. Like so many of the towns and villages in this part of Galicia it was largely destroyed by the French troops of Napoleon in the early 1800's but reminders of its historic past remain in the buildings and monuments and its narrow winding streets such as the typical Rúa Rosalía de Castro with the XVIIIthC facades of the Casa Mosteirín and adjoining Casa Mayá. Most of the restaurants and bars can be found around the wide Paseo Maritimo with the extensive modern shopping centre behind which is the newly located main bus station with regular services to and from Finisterre and Santiago.

[3] Detour ● ● ● ● **3.2** km by road (taxi?) to **Igrexa de Santiago da Ameixenda.** The church has a statue of St. James the Moor-slayer *Santiago Matamoros* and behind the main altar a small reliquary reputedly containing a piece of St. James finger(nail) extracted during the removal of his body from Dugium to Libredon and associated with yet more miracles in this deeply religious part of Galicia. A booklet entitled *Lenda de Santiago da Ameixenda* (in Spanish) is available from the church. Contact the Ayuntamiento in Cee to confirm opening hours. *Directions* to Ameixenda: From *Café Casa Talieiro* in **Os Camiños Chans** turn left along the main road over the bridge (Río de Brens) in Pontella [1.0 km] and turn off <left [1.5 km] up towards the village of Ameixenda. The church of Santiago is at the far end, so you need to continue for another [0.7 km] past the quaint bars and cafés and the Miracles Grocer *Ultramarinos Milagros*. On the outskirts of the town on Rua da Igrexa is *H* De Naturaleza © 645 823 993. Return the same way *or* continue to.

[4] Detour ● ● ● ● **11.4** km by road (8.2 km beyond Ameixenda to **Ézaro** Waterfall (taxi?). One of the most visited sites in Galicia and the only river *río Xallas* in Europe that flows directly into the sea as a waterfall. The Waterfall and Ézaro viewpoint are situated in a dramatic location at the foot of Mount Pindo (see under myths). Oficina de Información Turística O Ézaro (Dumbría) C/ Río do Barco © 662 346 927. Open all year. *CR* **Santa Uxía** © 981 106 664 + 3.5 km.

To continue to Corcubión / Finisterre – from the Cee option point* by albergue Moreira keep s/o down the steps to the *Paseo Maritimo* by the town beach *Praia da Concha* and up to the sign for Corcubión:

0.6 km **Corcubión** *Options* See town plan: [1] continue via the coast path adj. the main road (*yellow*). **[1a]** detour (add ½ km) to the beach and hotels in Praia de Quenxe (*turquoise*). **[2]** take the 'medieval' route through the old town (*dark blue*). **[3]** take the scenic upper path along the 'original' route above the town *(green)*. All routes join, after a steep climb, in San Roque c. 2½ km.

[1] ● ● ● ● continue by coast *paseo maritimo* parallel to the main road passing *H*****El Hórreo** €35 © 981 749 185 into **Praza de Castelao** with several bars and cafés. **Corcubión** an attractive seaside town designated a site of 'National Cultural Interest' with a (declining) population now 1,700 serving a busy summer tourist trade. Make your way up past the Taxi rank © 981 745 023 into calle de Castelao and up into Praza San Marcos with its fine XIIthC romanesque parish church ❶ **Igrexa San Marcos** [0.9 km] *gótico mariñeiro [Corcubión had extensive sea trade with Italy and Venice, hence the celebration of San Marcos].* Close by on Plaza Párroco Francisco Sánchez,3 *CR* **Casa de Bernarda** €30-60 © 981 747 157 m: 617 974 113.

[1a] ● ● ● ● From Praza San Marcos one can head back down to the *paseo maritimo* and Porto de Corcubión **Turismo** (summer) café *O Carrumeiro* and access the lovely sandy cove **Praia de Quenxe** ½ km off route with *H*ˢ **As Hortensias** €35+ ✆ 981 747 584 and *H*ˢ **Praia de Quenxe** €40-60 ✆ 981 706 457 with restaurants.

[2] ● ● ● ● For the 'medieval' route through the old town take the road up steeply by the Corcubión sign to pass *Alb.* ❺ **Camiño Fisterra** *Priv.[14÷1]* €10 ✆ 981 745 040 (Sinda) m: 629 114 122 c/ Cruceiro de Valdomar, 11 (same owner as Beiramar). Continue up and veer <left past viewpoint and into Rúa Rafael Juan to the welcoming *CR* **Casa da Balea** €40 ✆ 655 130 485 (Nº. 44). Continue down into **Praza de Castelao** passing Capilla del Pilar (right).

[3] ● ● ● ● For the upper route along woodland path above the town take the steps up right> directly *opposite* **Casa da Balea** up to the recently restored ❷ **Capela de San Antonio** *XVII.* Waymarks here are faded but continue along the concrete path by house Nº 14 (*not* up to Cuartel Gardia Civil). The concrete track levels off and skirts the side of the hill to rejoin the main route by the side of a stone wall.

[1] ● ● ● ● From ❶ **Igrexa San Marcos [0.9** km] continue up the steps right> into rua As Mercedes with well preserved houses bearing armorial shields into the wide square Campo do Rollo *[F.] Fuente Rollo Café*. Cross the square and head up the steep narrow lane to join wide track in the pine forest ahead (the alternative scenic route joins from the right). Continue up steeply to join an asphalt road turning right> into the hamlet of **Vilar [0.7** km] and proceed up to the top and over the main road for the final [0.6 km] to the windswept high point of this stage:

2.3 km   **Alto San Roque** *Vilar Alb.* **San Roque** *Asoc.[12÷1]* € donation ✆ 679 460 942 communal meal usually available (no local shops). Built with funds from the international relief effort from the Prestige oil disaster and managed by the *Associación Galician Amigos del Camino*.

The way now heads downhill playing hide-and-seek with the main road cutting off some of the sharp bends around the steep coastal inlets. Just beyond the albergue we pick up our first real view of the cape of Finisterre with the lighthouse (left) and the Monte Facho (right). The woodland path rejoins the main road at **Amarela** and continues for down to the beach at:

2.1 km   **Playa de Estorde** fine sandy bay with *H*ˢ **Playa de Estorde** ✆ 981 745 585 with café / restaurant and terrace overlooking the beach. Opposite *Ruta Finisterre Camping*. Continue along main road crossing over just before Sardiñeiro (or carry s/o down into the town):

1.0 km   **Sardiñeiro** The route crosses back over the main by *Hs* **Nicola** ✆ 981 743 741 with restaurant. Access the beach to the rear *Café A Cabaña* in seaside park also rear terrace of *Mesón Cabanel* (entrance main road). [Continue on main road (300m *off* route) to access *P*ˢ **Merendero** €12 (special pilgrim price) ✆ 981 743 535]. Continue back over main road (sign Praia do Rostro) up along narrow concrete road *rúa de Fisterra* through Sardiñero de Abaixo onto a woodland path that winds up through pine and eucalyptus plantation for a delightful stretch away from the main road to rejoin at:

Punto de Vista [2.0 km] wonderful viewpoint (weather dependant!) with unrestricted view of Cabo Finisterre (right) and Monte Pindo straight ahead across the bay. Cross the main road with care **[!]** at dangerous bend and enter a narrow path above the isolated beach of Talón (there are now steps down to this lovely isolated beach) and rejoin main road veering down <left on the laneway by a stone column marked *Corredoira de Don Camilo* and *H**** **Alén do Mar** €60-90 Ⓒ 981 740 745 modern luxury hotel set back from the beach in the woodland at Calcoba overlooking the delightful sandy beach **[1.1** km] at:

3.1 km   **Playa Langosteira** with its 2 kilometres of pure white sand.

> *Along a beach of dazzling white sand we advanced towards the cape, the bourne of our journey… it was upon this beach that, according to the tradition of all ancient Christendom, Saint James, the patron saint of Spain, preached the gospel to the heathen Spaniards. 'What is the name of this village?' said I to a woman as we passed by five or six ruinous houses at the bend of the bay, ere we entered upon the peninsular of Finisterre, 'This is no village, said the Gallegan, this is a city, this is Duyo.' So much for the glory of the world. These huts were all that the roaring sea and the tooth of time had left of Duyo, the great city! Onward now to Finisterre.* The Bible in Spain *George Borrow.*

Take off your boots and feel the sand on your feet? take a swim, laugh, cry or both – congratulations, you have arrived – well, almost! You are now 2.5 km from the centre of Finisterre (6 km from the lighthouse). If the weather is kind you can walk the beach alternatively take the waymarked route along the paved walkway through the pine trees directly ahead; parallel to the main road with

H*** **Playa Langosteira** €35-55 Ⓒ 981 706 830 in Anchoa and *H*** **Arenal** €35+ Ⓒ 981 740 644 Rúa Cabello (main road on outskirts of Finisterre). Both routes join at the far end of the beach at **San Roque** at the restaurant Tira do Cordell where you can watch the fishermen and women bringing their produce straight from the sea to the kitchen – expensive but exquisite (fish and mariscos doesn't come fresher than this). Adj. is another fish restaurant *P* **Doña Lubina** with rooms €35 Ⓒ 981 740 311. A concrete path brings us up past *Alb.*❶ **do Mar** *Priv.[18÷3]*+ €12 -€45 Ⓒ 981 740 204 on Rua S.Roque with terrace overlooking the sea. Pass viewpoint by wayside cross at **Baximar** from where we can look back over the sweeping curve of the Praia de Langosteira and the backdrop of mountains that brought us here.

Follow the main road past *H** **A Langosteira** €40 Ⓒ 981 740 543 Av. Coruña, 61 overlooking the sea and continue s/o (where the main road veers right) to pass *Alb.*❷ **A Cabo Vila** *Priv.[24÷1]*+ €12–€30 Ⓒ 981 740 454 m: 607 735 474 where Alexia, Nita & Alejandra await! Av. de A Coruña, 13, bajo. Just past the albergue is a turning (right – opp. Correos) to: *P** **López** Ⓒ 981 740 449 on Carasqueira. Continue past the local council offices *Concello de Fisterra* s/o down the narrow c/Santa Catalina past *P*** **Mariquito** €25-45 with bar/cafe and emerge at the central square with the municipal albergue on the corner opposite.

3.0 km **Finisterre** *Alb.* ❸ *Xunta[36÷2]*
€6 ✆ 981 740 781 original hostel on corner
of c/ Real (see photo right) well maintained
by the local council and ably managed by
Begoña and a team of volunteers. Open
from 13:00 which allows early arrivals
to shed their backpacks before exploring
the headland and lighthouse a further 3.5
km up the side of Monte Facho. Central
location close to all amenities and the bus-

stop for return journey to Santiago (unless you're planning to walk back via Muxia).
The albergue issues the certificate of completion *Fisterrana* to pilgrims who have
walked from Santiago (a stamped credencial essential) regardless of whether you are
staying in the hostel.

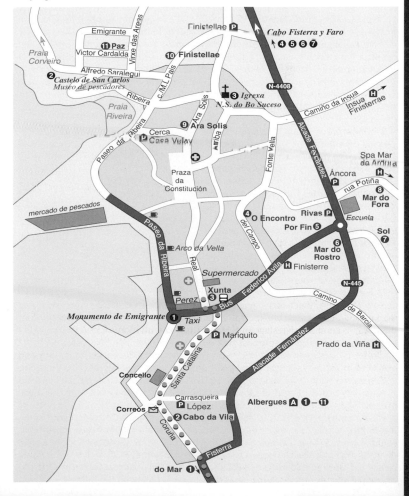

Other Albergues: ❹ **O Encontro** *Priv.[5÷1]* €12-15 © 696 503 363 c/del campo. ❺ **Por Fin** *Priv.[22÷4]* €10 © 636 764 726 c/Federico Avila,19 (run by Hungarian Aranka Rósa). ❻ **Mar do Rostro** *Priv.[23÷2]* €10 Pilar y Nazareth © 637 107 765 c/Alcade Fernandez,45. ❼ **Sol** *Priv.[22÷5]* €10-12 © 981 740 655 (Miguel) m: 617 568 648 c/ Atalaya,7 offering space for reflection and quiet garden. ❽ **Mar do Fora** *Priv.[10÷1]* €10 © 686 939 079 (Silvia y Dito) Rúa Potiña, 60 with terrace. ❾ **Ara Solis** *Priv.[16÷2]* €10-12 © 638 326 869 (Carlos Lagoa) c/Ara Solis,3. ●(10) **Finistellae** *Priv.[20÷2]* €12 © 661 493 505 c/ Manuel Lago Pais,7. ●(11) **Paz** *Priv. [30÷7]* €10 © 981 740 332 (Enrique) m: 628 903 693 c/ Victor Cardalda,11.

Other hotels & pensions: © 981 740 044. *H*° **Finisterre** © 981 740 000 €35 Federico Ávila. *P*°° **Rivas** €20-40 © 981 740 027 Rúa Alcalde Fernández, 53 on main roundabout. *H*° **Áncora** €27-49 © 981 740 791 c/Alcalde Fernández, 43. *H*°°**Prado da Vina** €35 © 981 740 326 Camino da Barcia. *P*° **Casa Velay** Rúa (Plaza) de Cerca © 981 740 127. *P*° **Fin da Terra** c/Atalaia © 981 712 030 + **Mirador** montarón. *H*°° **Rústico Ínsua Finisterrae** €35-75 © 981 712 211 camino Insua, 128 near back beach and *H Spa* **Mar da Ardora** 981 740 590 c/ Potiña. *H*°° **O Semáforo** © 981 725 869 adj. lighthouse (often closed). *Restaurants:* are plentiful with fresh fish and shellfish *mariscos* a speciality. The ubiquitous TV and harsh neon lighting doesn't help the ambience but Tira do Cordel at Baixamar comes closest to the authentic gastronomic experience but there is plenty of competition. Amongst the best value is Mesón Arco da Vella on Paseo da Ribeira with home cooking from Carmen and a first floor terrace overlooking the harbour (arrive early if you want a table).

The municipal albergue dovetails as the *Oficina de Turismo* on Rúa Real,2 © 981 740 781. The main bus stop is adjacent with 5 buses daily to Santiago between 08:20 and 19:00 travel time 3 hours ± €12 depending on route) *Castromil / Monbus* © 902 292 900. Taxi Central: Cándido © 630 138 828 (Santiago 1½ ± hours €90).
Finisterre is a busy fishing port with a resident population of 5,000. This number swells during the summer months as tourists and pilgrims converge on the town with its range of shops, bars, restaurants and hotels. While the town is sheltered

from the worst of the westerly gales it has nevertheless been ravaged by wind, rain and pirates down through the centuries, consequently there is little of historic or artistic significance remaining. However the town's somewhat 'untidy' layout and modernity overlies a rich historical past.

Note: If you have walked from Olveiroa you will likely want to shower and rest before tackling (perhaps the next day) the 9.9 km round-trip of Cabo Finisterre including the famous lighthouse (now a popular tourist attraction) but the headland also invites exploration of the less well known historic and mythical sites. Each specific spot has a number that corresponds to its location on the map so you can readily identify each one. Your decision might rest on practical realities such as the state of the weather. If you are blessed with a clear sky it may be worth the effort to join the crowds at the lighthouse or climb Monte Facho or the less strenuous option to walk over to the back-beach, the Outer Sea *Mar de Fora* to watch the sun sink below the Western horizon… or take a tour of the town, have a drink with friends, or both? Descriptions of these various options are detailed on the following pages.

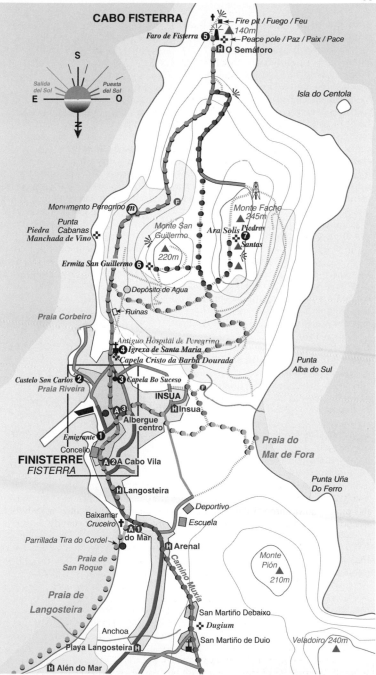

CABO FISTERRA

Fire pit / Fuego / Feu

▲ 140m

Peace pole / Paz / Paix / Pace

Faro de Fisterra **5**

🅗 O Semáforo

Isla do Centola

Monumento Peregrino (m)

Punta
Piedra   Cabanas
Manchada de Vino

🄵

Monte Facho
▲ 245m

Monte San
Guillermo

Ara Solis

Piedras

7

Santas

▲ 220m

Ermita San Guillermo **6**

Depósito de Agua

Praia Corbeiro

Ruinas

Antiguo Hospital de Peregrino

✝**4** Igrexa de Santa Maria

Capela Cristo da Barba Dourada

Punta
Alba do Sul

Castelo San Carlos **2**
Praia Riveira

3 Capela Bo Suceso

INSUA

🅐 **3**

🅗 Insua

Albergue
centro

Emigrante **1**

Concello

FINISTERRE
FISTERRA

🅐**2** A Cabo Vila

Praia do
Mar de Fora

Punta Uña
Do Ferro

🅗 Langosteira

Baixamar
Cruceiro

Deportivo

Escuela

✝🅐**1**
do Mar

🅗 Arenal

Parrillada Tira do Cordel

Monte
Pión
▲ 210m

*Praia de
San Roque*

*Praia de
Langosteira*

Camino Muxia

Anchoa

San Martiño Debaixo

Dugium

Veladoiro 240m ▲

Playa Langosteira 🅗

San Martiño de Duio

🅗 Alén do Mar

S
E   O
Salida
del Sol
Puesta
del Sol

Town Centre and Charles Fort 1.0 km *(round trip).* Allow a couple of hours for a leisurely stroll around the lively harbour area. From the albergue pass the evocative Monument to the Emigrant ❶ *Monumento de Emigrante* (see photo right with rising sun over Monte Pindo) and continue down to the fish market *Mercado de Pescado* resembling the lines of Finisterre's modern fishing fleet. You can visit the fish market and information display on the first floor (small entrance fee). Continue along the sea front to the austere fortified tower of Harbour House overlooking the town beach *Praia de Ribeira* with St. Charles Castle ❷ *Castelo de San Carlos XVIII* located above the entrance to the sandy bay. This strategic was recently converted to a fishing museum *museo de pescadores* with artefacts and historical information recognising the importance of the fishing industry to this part of Galicia. The canon a stark reminder of its military past. Not many continue to the viewpoint located behind the fort that overlooks the tiny cove *Praia Corbeiro* with delightful beach for swimming.

It is delightfully easy to get lost in the narrow back lanes but the sea is never far away so you might return via the baroque chapel of the Good Event ❸ *Capela do Bo Suceso XVII* located at the original heart of the town in Sun-Altar Square *Praza Ara-Solis*. Here we also find Quadrant House that dates from the 13th C and was reputedly an ancient pilgrim hospital. Continue back along Calle de la Ara-Solis to Constitution Square *Plaza da Constitución* and return to the municipal albergue in the centre via the Royal Way *Calle del Real*.

Cabo Finisterre – 3.5 km *(9.9 km round trip via Monte Facho)*: You can of course take any number of alternative routes but the one described here covers the main sites of historic, religious and mythological interest in the shortest distance, commencing with a hike up the asphalt road to the lighthouse and returning via peaceful woodland paths. Allow half a day for the recommended round trip of steep hilly ground. If you intend to make a thanksgiving or purification ritual then consider staying an extra day as there is much to see and do. Remember it is 3.5 km just to the lighthouse (7.0 km there and back). Note the numbered sites ❶ to ❼ refer to the detailed notes on mythology and are linked to the map of Cabo Finisterre to aid identification.

Leave the albergue up the narrow Calle Real and through the main square Plaza de la Constitución veering right> into the Plaza Ara Solis and <left at the 17th century seafaring chapel *Capela do Bo Suceso* **[0.4 km]** up to join the main road just below the church of Our Lady of the Sands ❹ *Igrexa de Santa María das Areas* **[0.5 km]**. This 12th C Romanesque church is a religious and historical gem (see photo right). Like so many churches today it is often locked but it is worth

the effort to check opening times. Inside is the chapel of Christ of the Golden Beard *Cristo da Barba Dourada* ✤ *(see Myths and Legends)* and a fine statue of *Santiago Peregrino* St James the Pilgrim in the nave. To the rear is the cemetery and the arched remains of the last pilgrim refuge in medieval Christendom. Perhaps you will rest awhile on the stone seating that surrounds the church and take time to pay tribute to the pilgrims who made it to the end of the world – many didn't as pilgrim cemeteries all the way from France attest. Here Christian monks welcomed and cared for the exhausted pilgrim from as early as the 11th century – a place, perhaps, to give thanks for your own safe arrival.

Continue uphill past turn-off right> **[0.6 km]** *[short-cut to the top of Monte Facho]* and s/o up the asphalt road past statue of a medieval pilgrim opposite the *Fonte Cabanas* **[0.5 km]** whose clear spring waters gush out of the side of Monte Facho and into the sea at *Cabanas* the rocky cove below and site of another legend linking Christ with Finisterre *Piedra Manchada de Vino* ✤. It's now a climb to the turn-off (right) **[0.9 km]** to Monte Facho but keep s/o past the souvenir shops, a bar and the marine observatory (now converted to hotel **O Semáforo**) to lighthouse **[0.5 km]**.

3.5 km ❺ Lighthouse *Faro* the famed lighthouse at the 'end of the world' has likewise been refurbished and is now a museum and exhibition space with audio-visual display on the history of Finisterre and its peoples. With the advent of satellite navigation systems the lighthouse is largely redundant although it remains a tracking station for shipping. Outside are various monuments to the 'discovery' of the Americas by European explorers. The most recent and uplifting addition (above the lighthouse) is a *Peace Pole* ✤ planted by the international World Peace Project. Its simple message reads, 'May Peace Prevail On Earth' *Que La Paz Prevalezca En La Tierra* and points heavenward encouraging us to 'think peace to create peace'.

Just below and to the rear of the lighthouse are several pilgrim monuments including the poignant brass boot rooted in the rock face and surrounded by the Atlantic swell that crashes around the headland 126 metres (413 feet) below. The pungent smell, blackened rocks and adjoining fire pit are evidence of 'burnt offerings' left by modern-day pilgrims. A common ritual is to burn an item of old clothing or some written statement that includes attachments or habits no longer wanted or needed and to see the ashes of our past actions blown away so that, like the Phoenix, we can arise anew and fly to ever greater heights.

When you feel complete with your lighthouse visit make your way back to the souvenir stalls and take the shortcut across the carpark to join the upper road that climbs steeply to earth track straight ahead and *option* **[1.2 km] [a]** continue up the asphalt road to radio mast and Monte Facho **[0.8 km]** or **[b]** take the track that keeps the contour line between Monte Facho (left) and Monte San Guillermo (right) and turn right> onto *path* **[0.7 km]** through the gorse that covers much of this modest rise known as *Monte San Guillermo* ✤ **[0.3 km]**:

2.3 km ❻ Saint William's Hermitage 5[th]century *Ermita de San Guillerme* 221m (725 feet). This wonderful hermitage site is little visited excepting periodical archaeological investigation but this is unobtrusive and leaves the area largely intact. Take care not to disturb the ancient stonewalls and respect this ancient sacred site. The hermitage is a bare ruin built into the leeward side of the giant boulder sheltering it from the strong Westerly winds that roar across this headland, protecting it too from the pagan rites associated with Monte Facho. Here the hermitage faces due East to catch the first rays of the rising sun over the Celtic 'Mount Olympus' *Monte Pindo* (see photo right). Several sources state that St. James himself preached from this spot in his efforts to counter the pagan rites associated with the *Ara Solis* (see Mythology) and the subsequent fertility rites practised here.

To access Monte Facho and the *Sacred Stones Piedras Santas* ❖ return to the main track **[0.3** km] turn right> and continue down to a fire break through the pine woods up on your <left **[0.3** km] make your way up rough track for **[0.4** km] to:

1.0 km ❼ **Piedras Santas** Here at 240 metres (787 feet) above sea level is an uninterrupted view west over the Atlantic with the horizon at this height around 56 kilometres (35 miles). There are 3 rocky outcrops spread out along the wide forestry track that collectively make up the Sacred Stones *Piedras Santas* and the Sun Altar *Ara Solis* ❖. The small island just offshore to the south/west is named after the Spider Crab *Centola* also linked to a pagan myth. *Alternative return routes from Monte Facho to the town centre:*

[a] 4.4 km – This is longest route but worth considering if visibility is poor as it follows the asphalt road from the wireless station at the southern end of Monte Facho and returns via the lighthouse road but it is exposed to wind and rain.

[b] 2.9 km – a shorter more sheltered route is to return via a wide woodland track to rejoin the asphalt road above the church of Santa Maria. Make your way back down the firebreak to the dirt track below and turn <left and imm. right> at the fork [0.4 km] ❖ where the wide forest track runs gently down past the town's water supply and continues back down to rejoin the main road [1.1 km] to pass the church of Santa Maria and back to the town centre [1.4 km].

[c] 3.1 km – *[1.7 Praia do Mar de Fora + 1.4 km back to Finisterre] (via the back beach or 'outer sea' – Praia do Mar de Fora):* Make your way back down the firebreak to the dirt track below and turn <left and s/o at the fork [0.4 km] ❖ *(ignoring the right-hand track described at [b] above)* continue to second wide sweep left [0.3 km] [!] at this point you leave the main track and take the narrow

stone-lined path that drops steeply down. This was an original access way to Monte Facho and it certainly has an ancient feel about it. Continue down to the top end of the straggling village of **A Insua** [0.5 km] to Europe's quirkiest shop on the corner (right). *(At this point you can continue s/o back to the centre of Finisterre)* or turn <left at small concrete parking area onto paved footpath (passing the ancient *Fonte Cardal* left – 50m *off* the path) and turn

<left [200m] onto boardwalk to viewpoint above the beach [300m]. Make your way down to the delightful windswept sand and the ocean.

Note: It is dangerous to swim in the unpredictable currents that sweep around this headland and take care if paddling in the shallows as there can be a surprisingly strong undertow – but otherwise enjoy the wild and generally deserted environment. In bygone days, before the lighthouse was built, pilgrims would come here to ritually cleanse themselves. The blood, sweat and tears that you may have shed along the way are part of our individual and collective purification. Fire and water were also associated with purification and rebirth. An ancient rite, followed by some modern pilgrims, involved burning one's old clothes and donning fresh garments as an act of renewal. Recycling, rather than burning, might be an environmentally responsible modification. An endearing ritual here also involved kneeling (not swimming) in the shallows and allowing nine waves to wash over the body – representing a rebirth into a new life washed clean by spirit. No one needs permission to devise their own rituals provided their focus is love and they are performed discreetly and safely with due respect to the traditional environment in which they are offered. Pilgrims now mostly come here to simply celebrate life in this beautiful spot away from the crowds.

From here there are several ways back to the town centre and the pilgrim hostel. The most direct route is via the hamlet of **A Insua** (now effectively a suburb of Finisterre). Make your way back along the path you originally came down but carry s/o at the first turning (now on your right) [0.3 km] and follow the path up to the asphalt road (new buildings) and turn right> [0.2 km] and <left at T-junction [0.2 km] *(The Hotel Rústico Insua is up to your right)* and take this road all the way down to main roundabout by Hotel Ancora and the primary school [0.5 km] and s/o down to the town centre [0.2 km]. *(note: An alternative path leads past the sport hall deportivo to the Arenal / Baixamar district at the north end of town).*

Finisterre: Myths & Legends:

Finisterre *Finis-Terrae* translates simply as Lands-End or 'End of the World'. From prehistoric times right up to the Middle Ages this was, quite literally, the end of the known world. It was here, at this very point, that the material world – the world of matter, seen with the physical eye, met the world of spirit that could only be seen with spiritual vision. In our increasingly materialistic culture the clash of these two worlds takes on new meaning and import. Over countless millennia Finisterre has provided a dramatic focal point for this theatre of contention – which keeps faith, as Goethe says; *with the world of things and the world of spirits equally.*

Finisterre's symbolic significance and potency is not lost on the pilgrims who still come here seeking to reconcile this conflict of inner and outer realities in their lives. This guidebook seeks, however inadequately, to find a balance between these 'outer' and 'inner' worlds. The following notes relate to the fascinating culture of Galicia and a rough guide to the mythology and significance of Finisterre as both a modern and ancient pilgrim destination. Much has been written concerning Celtic mythology and the abiding mysticism and practises of the ancient Druids. While travelling through Galicia, George Borrow writes in *The Bible in Spain – The Druid's Stone:*

> *I observed a pile of stones of rather a singular appearance… it was a Druidical altar, and the most perfect and beautiful one of the kind I had ever seen. It was circular, and consisted of stones immensely large and heavy at the bottom, which towards the top became thinner, having been fashioned by the hand of art to something of the shape of scollop shells... I gazed with reverence and awe upon the pile where the first colonies of Europe offered their worship to the unknown God. The temples of the mighty and skilful Roman, comparatively of modern date, have crumbled to dust in its neighbourhood. The Roman has left behind him his deathless writings, his history, and his songs; the Goth his liturgy, his traditions, and the germs of noble institutions; the Moor his chivalry, his discoveries in medicine, and the foundations of the modern commerce; and where is the memorial of the Druidic races? Yonder: that pile of eternal stones!*

Here, since prehistoric times, people had come to worship some Great Force beyond human understanding, a power that spoke of eternity and enlightenment based on the perennial light of the sun. This precise spot became one of the holiest and most revered in the ancient world. We can imagine the Altar to the Sun *Ara Solis* being both a physical and symbolic point of veneration, a place of sacred worship to a transcendent power. There could have been no richer seam of potential converts for the Christian cause than this. The following legendary sites are marked on the map of Cabo Finisterre so you can readily identify them.

The *Ara Solis* and the sacred stones *Piedras Santas* became natural altars for the ancient rites where the 'world of things and the world of spirits' met. Such was the significance of this site, that the Romans built here the legendary city of Dugium *(Dugio /Duyo /Duio)*. It is said that legionnaires retired here to end their days where they were closest to the 'meeting of the worlds' and paradise itself. This is, perhaps, a reference to the Elysian Fields mentioned by the Roman historian Estrabon as, 'a peaceful place, where once dead heroes and those favoured by the gods found rest… a place in the far west, at the confines of the earth, where the sun hid.' Benjamín Trillo Trillo in *As Pegadas de Santiago na Cultura de Fisterra* goes further suggesting that Finisterre was the original and favoured place for the burial of St. James:

> *The route of Saint James is in reality the route of the west, the one followed by the sun on its way to sunset [where] the mansion of pious souls can be found… We cannot forget the explicit naming of the town of Duio in the Liber Sancti Jacobi, nor that the king of the town prevented the disciples of Saint James from burying his body in the surroundings of Fisterra. For this reason we can understand perfectly why the pilgrims, who for many centuries went to the town of Compostela, would also want to visit Fisterra, in order to see among other things the place where the body of the apostle should have been buried if the devil had not prevented it.*

Thankfully, little remains to authenticate the historical origins of Duio and so it lives on in legend far more forcefully than if it were just another tourist site. The nearby village of Duio San Martiño still evokes a timelessness not marred by souvenir shops. We have already mentioned how the early Christian Church sought out the sacred sites of pagans and Druids in order to graft its own message directly onto these cultures. Any area that held spiritual significance was the logical place to endeavour to weave a new consciousness. It is therefore entirely reasonable to assume that Saint James would have come *specifically* to Finisterre as one of the foremost sites of spiritual practise and ritual in the then known world. More speculative is the notion that he may, in turn, have been following in the footsteps of his Master.

Legends abound of Jesus travelling with Joseph of Aramathea to visit Druidic teachers in Cornwall. It has already been suggested that Joseph earned his wealth from trading in tin and importing it to Palestine from the mines in Britannia. The Phoenicians and Romans had opened a sea route between the two countries the previous century and this route went directly past the Roman seaport of *Artabrorum Portus* mentioned by Ptolemy and described as, '…a large port serving an intense trading activity,' that scholars have identified as the port of Finisterre. This is corroborated by the writings of George Borrow who described the port as, "… echoing with a thousand voices when the ships and trade of all known lands met in Duio." There is general agreement that the present day hamlet of San Martiño de Duio is the Duio referred to and this in turn derives from the Roman town of Dugium built on the site of a former Celtic Citania here.

❹ ✣ Christ of the Golden Beard *Cristo da Barba Dourada.* If Christ Jesus travelled to Britannia during the 18 years when we know nothing of his whereabouts he would have sailed right past this headland and it would be reasonable to assume that his ship would have gone ashore for provisions. In such a case it would be inconceivable that Jesus did not meet with the Druidic masters who served this most important centre of spiritual initiation. It is interesting that the figure of Jesus continues to play such an important part in the customs of modern day Finisterre. Miracles have always been associated with the remarkably beautiful effigy of Christ on the Cross that hangs in the ancient parish Church of Santa Maria. This image is said to have been created by Nicodemus who, along with Joseph

of Aramathea prepared the body of Jesus for burial. This beautiful figure known and revered as 'The Christ of the Golden Beard' *Cristo da Barba Dourada* has long been associated with miraculous powers of healing and a commonly held belief was that the body perspired and the beard was seen to grow.

How this statue came to reside in Finisterre has become a legend in itself that bears a similarity to the story of Jesus calming the waters in Galilee. A ship sailing to England encountered a storm while passing Finisterre and would have foundered had not the crew thrown the figure of Christ into the waters whereupon they became miraculously calmed.

The highlight of the religious calendar in Finisterre is Holy Week celebrated each year with a moving re-enactment of Christ's death, burial and resurrection when a white dove is released symbolising the Holy Spirit ascending into heaven.

This annual festival draws thousands of people from all over Spain and is designated of national importance. The threads that connect Jesus with Finisterre may be tenuous but they exist and just as the 33 stages along the French Way *Camino Francés* can be experienced as the thirty three years of Christ's life, so too can the 3 stages to Finisterre be likened to his death and resurrection.

❖ **The Wine Stained Rock** *Piedra Manchada de Vino.* The relatively inaccessible cove of **Cabanas** faces east towards Monte Pindo and here we find another of the many legends associating Christ with Finisterre. Jesus is said to have appeared at this spot to hold back the waters threatening to submerge the town. It was also here that San Guillerme (whose hermitage lies above the road at this point) met with sailors at Cabanas who gave him a barrel of wine that he tried to carry back up the steep slope. The devil, disguised as a peasant, offered to help but dragged him backwards smashing the cask on the rocks below which became red – thus birthing the legend of the wine-stained rock *piedra manchada de vino* this being an allegory to the blood of Christ spilt for our redemption as celebrated in the Eucharist – there are references to mass being offered at this spot in bygone times. It is also the place where the figure of Christ and his statue were said to have been washed ashore. Above the site is the modern burial ground *cementerio (casa de todos los muertos).*

The legends surrounding St. James give wonderfully descriptive portrayals of his death and burial in Galicia. But few direct their attention to why he came initially to Galicia to preach and why his body was returned to an obscure area known as Libredon. Padrón is popularly identified as the town where he first set foot in Galicia to preach the gospel and to which his body was returned for burial. We have already seen that Finisterre was one of the most powerful places of ancient worship and spiritual initiation in the known-world and it lies a mere days sail from Padrón and 3 days walk from Santiago. Those tenuous threads that link Jesus with Finisterre become much stronger in linking St. James with this headland. While Padrón was well established as a trading port so was Dugium which, in addition, had the essential spiritual significance. Finisterre was the ideal and logical destination.

✤ **Lighthouse *Faro* Peace Pole & Fire-Pit.** Owing to its pagan past Finisterre has been largely excluded from the Santiago story. But this exclusion has allowed Finisterre the freedom to become a beacon of light to welcome all people in its universal embrace. This inclusivity is evidenced by the planting of one of the first Peace Poles in Spain into the solid rock of Cabo Finisterre. This internationally recognised symbol of the hopes and dreams of the entire human family stands vigil in silent prayer for universal peace and adjoins the lighthouse. An identical pole lies at the site of the baptism of Jesus on the Jordan. Finisterre has always been a link between east and west – between inner and outer authority. The Way to Finisterre affords us an opportunity to let go out-worn belief systems based on fear, guilt and separation. Once we have dispensed with limiting prejudice and dogma we become open and ready to receive a new wisdom based on inclusivity and cooperation. So

here, behind the lighthouse, an ancient pilgrim rite has been revived. The local council has provided a fire-pit so that pilgrims can burn an item of old clothing or other token to represent the letting-go of the old in order to awaken to the new. Remember this is a symbolic gesture and doesn't require the burning of an entire wardrobe! An old sock or a simple handwritten note will do perfectly.

Having played its part in the establishment of Christianity in Europe, acting as a magnet for the first Christian missionaries, Finisterre may yet have a role in the unfolding of a new epoch – one less dependent on the idea of a 'chosen people' and embracing all of humanity. A time when we begin to understand that if God is our Father then we are each a part of His Sonship. Jesus was crucified for proclaiming this heretical idea. But the desire for specialness based on exclusion has been the greatest cause of war and suffering in the human story. Until we focus on what connects us rather than what divides us we will never find lasting peace in our world. From the Human Rights movement sprang the phrase, 'All men and women are created equal' but we have yet to find the courage to live out that noble truth. Perhaps the path to the 'end of the way and the world' will yet become a starting point for a new consciousness based on unconditional love of God, neighbour and self.

✤ **Hermitage of Saint William *Ermita de San Guillerme*.** So, having arrived in the present and peeked into the future we return to the past and make our way to the 5[th]C hermitage of Saint William located on a site that St. James himself is said to have preached from in his attempt to discredit the pagan rituals practised at the nearby *Ara Solis*. This is easier to understand if we remember that the Christ Light, with its promise of a New Jerusalem, arose in the east. Trillo Trillo states:

> *The hermitage, associated both with Saint James and the Ara Solis, was the ideal place to find Christ in the Middle Ages [and] there is a clear relationship between the Hermitage of San Guillerme and the Resurrection of Christ in the Christian tradition: the heathens believed in the fertility powers of the Ara Solis whilst the Christians believed in the saving grace of Christ. Immortality is not achieved through reproduction, but by the resurrection.*

But it is also clear that the lines between paganism and Christianity are often smudged. San Guillerme's 'bed' a stone plinth with its shallow depression has long been associated with miraculous powers of fertility and drew infertile couples to 'lie together' on its surface in their desire to conceive, aided by the powers of the saint himself. Ancient fertility rites have long been associated with this headland. There is also some confusion as to whom San Guillerme actually was. Some

sources suggest he was none other than Saint Guillerme le Désert the French hermit who founded the pilgrimage centre on the Arles camino built around a fragment of the True Cross. Perhaps most understood him simply as a holy man who lived a devout life based on Christ's teaching. It is certainly a remote and peaceful spot – its isolated position still protecting it from the modern day-tripper visiting the lighthouse. Above the hermitage, at the top of the Monte de San Guillerme, is one of several sites associated with the Ara Solis. Wherever its exact position it is clear that all pagan altars will have been systematically destroyed by the newly emerging Christian religion.

❖ **Monte Facho** *Ara Solis:* The first references to the Sun Temple *Ara Solis* came from the Romans who, when they arrived here in the 1st century BC, came across the Phoenician altar and witnessed a thriving place of worship and initiation. While there is some difference in opinion as to the exact location of 'the' altar to some extent the entire headland must have acted as a sacred site and would have been used in its entirety in ceremonial processions and worship. Whatever of the

pagan rites practised here over the centuries one (Christian) interpretation is that the horizon represented the lip of the Chalice, a symbol of the Holy Grail itself, and the sun represented the Host – a symbolic representation that forms the emblem of Galicia today which incorporates a chalice with host above it surrounded by seven crosses representing the seven historical cities of Galicia – coincidentally there are also seven Celtic tribes. The highest spot on the headland was inevitably a place of major significance. It is here that we find the Holy Stones *Piedras Santas* and a location for the *Ara Solis* with access opposite the *Piedra del Carballo de Oro*.

Perhaps you will be able to locate the Rocking Stone *Abalar* and have the experience of moving 10 tons of solid granite with your own hand, *"If ye have faith as a grain of mustard seed, ye shall say to this mountain, move hence to yonder place; and it shall move and nothing shall be impossible unto you."* Or From the diaries of the 16thC German pilgrim Erich Lassota, we read:

... at the Fisterra headland summit, at the mountain called Facho, we can find the Pedras Santas. The Holy Stones are two big and almost round stones on which the people conferred certain gifts. It is said that over them rested Our Lady. These stones, even that you can't move them back using several oxen teams, are easy to move with a finger, a fact that I established for myself.

A Christian myth tells of the Virgin Mary resting over these stones but pagan worshippers had a very different interpretation. Here we can see how a prior pagan initiation rite was erased from popular memory by the substitution of a new Christian legend. It is said the Virgin appeared here to encourage St. James in his ministry. But it is not generally known that these stones are easily moved *abalar* and were allegedly the site of an earlier pagan rite whereby the movement of the stones proved (or disproved) the virginity of a priestess before she was allowed to perform certain ceremonial duties. The phrase 'to put her over the stone' was a reference to this ordeal. What better way to extinguish such references to this ancient practise but by instigating a new legend whereby the Virgin Mary appeared in this selfsame spot to support the ministry of St. James. A parallel pagan practise and similar substitution took place at Muxía (see later).

The small island just offshore to the south/west is named after the Spider Crab *Centola* found at Finisterre and associated with the abode of the devil. The Christian church often promulgated fearful myths of devil worship associated with paganism in order to frighten superstitious locals from cavorting with the heathens. One such classic tale relates to the witch Orcavella who is said to have seduced unwary young men into her snake-ridden cave and 'smothered' them to death with her embrace. Just in case the younger generation should show interest in these pagan rituals – she was known to eat children as well. Further exploration is discouraged as her cave is said to lie behind the fence surrounding the wireless station.

❖ **Orcavella's Tomb** *Tomba de Orcavella*. There are several sources that relate the legend of the witch Orcavella who lived in a cave on Monte Facho. The following is a shortened extract from *O Camiño de Fisterra* by Fernando Alonso Romero and refers to the *Silva Curiosa* published in Paris in 1583 wherein the knight Medrano describes his pilgrimage to Fisterra and the story told him by a hermit there. This hermit described the existence of an ancient sepulchre 'in a deserted and isolated place near which were some large high rocks'. The knight went to investigate and as he approached the place a shepherd came running and shouting:

> *Keep away! Keep away! Good Lord, brother, where are you going? Do you want to perish? Do you not know that amongst those rocks there is enclosed the damned body of the enchantress Orcabella, and that every man or woman who ever set eyes upon her has died within a year? She could make herself invisible and robbed and ate as many children she had a mind to... and left half the kingdom depopulated. When she got tired of living, she withdrew to these crags and in one of them she carved out her tomb. With the help of a shepherd whom she kept a spellbound prisoner, she raised up a big tombstone to cover the sepulchre and slid it on the opening to cover it. Afterwards she undressed and embracing the sad shepherd and in payment of all the services he had rendered her, she threw him into the sepulchre and shut him in there. She, leaving her clothes outside, got into this deadly bed, and using the unfortunate shepherd as a mattress, lay on top of him... the unlucky shepherd shouted and screamed so much that the other shepherds who were in that bleak place, ran to where the shouts came from and were surprised and frightened to see that the sepulchre was completely surrounded by snakes and serpents.*

❖ **Dugium** *San Martino de Duio* There is nothing to actually 'see' of Dugium and only limited archaeological investigations have taken place in the area. Trillo Trillo cites Aldao Carré as follows:

Dugium was no myth: the considerable remains of dwellings and other objects to be found in this area are proof of this… sometimes flint axe heads and bevelled copper spearheads and sometimes brick pavements and the remains of Roman pottery, all of which stands as proof that two different civilisations passed through there. The city must have been very large judging by the distances between the different points where such articles are to be found… it would therefore appear quite clear that there did exist a Romanized hill fort civilisation living in the Duio valley with a large port serving an intense trading activity.

The legendary site of **Dugium (Duio)** lies [2.3 km] North of Finisterre on the path to Muxía so if you are continuing on that route you pass right through the area. However if you want to independently visit the Duio valley (with its lovely views back over Finisterre and Langosteira beach) then follow the path to Muxía past the Baixamar cross and viewpoint that looks across towards Duio and continue as far as the crossroads at **Escaselas** [3.0 km]. To return to Finisterre via Langosteira beach turn right> and

crossover the main road C-550 [0.4 km] beside the modern Hotel Playa Langosteira and take the grass access lane direct to the beach path. From here it is [1.7 km] back to the town centre for a total round trip of 5.1 km. Or turn up left into **Hermedesuxo** (½ km further on the waymarked route to Muxía) *Note*: Hermedesuxo is the site of an intriguing hypothesis put forward by the knowledgeable Trillo Trillo as follows:

The existence of such a city [Dugium] with the characteristics already discussed begs the question: Who was or were the religious deities who protected it? Hermes was the god of traders and also had links with the fertility myth. I mention [this] link because there is a place called Hermedesujo in the valley of Duio. In a XIIth Century document… Hermedesujo de Abajo appears as 'Hermo'… Although the usual linguistic interpretation of the word Hermo would be 'an uninhabitable place', such an explanation does not fit with the facts. And it is for this reason that one should not rule out the possibility this place, once called Hermes was later turned into Hermo owing to Christianity's eagerness to demystify local place names. Murguía adds: 'Let us not forget the pyschopompic Hermes [was also] the soul bearer.

Continuing the ever popular theme of death and dying is the ominous name given to this entire coastline – **Coast of Death Costa da Morte** a reference, perhaps, to the cult of the dead or the Celtic Otherworld than to its manifold shipwrecks. Due west of Duio lies Ship Headland *Cabo de Nave* with its allusion to the boat that carries the souls of the dead to the Underworld ruled over by Hades. The headland here together with the small island directly off it *Berrón da Nave* looks like a helmeted Roman soldier (when viewed from Monte Facho) – his body laid to rest with his head lying to the west. Even George Borrow becomes somewhat mournful as he arrives at the Costa da Morte and writes:

It was not without reason that the Latins gave the name of Finis Terrae to this district… the termination of the world, beyond which there was a wild sea, or abyss, or chaos... those moors and wilds, over which I have passed, are the rough and dreary journey of life. Cheered with hope, we struggle through all the difficulties of moor, bog and mountain, to arrive at – what? The grave and its dreary sides. Oh, may hope not desert us in the last hour – hope in the Redeemer and in God!'

This wild headland is often shrouded in sea mist but it is these myths of old that fascinate and continue to draw us here. It is, perhaps, a pity that factual records of these pagan, Phoenician, Celtic and Roman rites have been largely erased from the history books. The early Christian church, no doubt threatened by the ideas behind worship of the sun and the notion of *Tir-na-Nóg*, suppressed what information was available. Today we can only marvel at the zeal of early pilgrims, Christian and pre-Christian, that risked life and limb to travel to this remote corner of the Earth. It is likely that interest in this legendary headland will draw ever-increasing numbers to visit. It is important to respect the sacred nature of this landscape and to keep the area free of litter and celebration parties – let's keep the wine and beer to the bar or beach and don't let irritation at disrespectful behaviour allow us to leave behind the psychic rubbish of superiority or resentment!

We would do well to remember that our rituals are symbolic of some greater understanding and the most important thing is to find a place where we can feel at peace to connect to that deeper wisdom. The actual rock or earth upon which we carry out our chosen ritual, prayer or meditation is immaterial – it is the energy of love that makes the ceremony sacred, not the place. The mystical notes from stage one cautioned us not to confuse sacred sites with insight and A Course In Miracles reminds us that the true temple is not a structure at all – its holiness lies at the inner altar whose beauty cannot be seen with the physical eye. An emphasis on beautiful structures can be a sign of unwillingness to exercise spiritual vision.

Countless thousands have travelled to Finisterre over millennia as witness to some force beyond our understanding. Overlooking the harbour at the end of our journey is the haunting monument to the emigrant. As we arrive at the end of the world it is perhaps humbling to recall the thousands that departed from this selfsame spot to start their own journey of discovery of a brave 'New World.'

> We shall not cease from exploration
> And the end of all our exploring
> Will be to arrive where we started
> And know the place for the first time.
>
> Four Quartets, *T.S. Eliot*

❏ **Regret for the things we did can be tempered by time.**
It is regret for the things we did not do that is inconsolable. *Sidney Harris*

4 FINISTERRE (*FISTERRA*) – MUXÍA

....	--- ---	13.7	--- ---	*49%*
▬▬▬	--- ---	14.4	--- ---	*51%*
▬▬▬	--- ---	0.0	--- ---	*0%*
Total km		**28.1** km (17.5 ml)		

30.8 km (^ 540m = 2.7 km)
Alto ▲ Monte Lourido 270m (885 ft)
<🅰 🅷> San Salvador **4.2** km – Buxan **6.8** km – Lires **13.5** km – Frixe **15.5** km

[Elevation profile: 300m / 200m gridlines. FINISTERRE, S.Salvador, Buxan, Castrexe, Lires, Frixe, Morquintián, Monte Lourido Alto 270m, Lourido, MUXÍA. Scale: 00 km, 5 km, 10 km, 15 km, 20 km, 25 km]

❏ **The Practical Path:** Delightful forest paths and farm tracks offering shade and shelter from the unpredictable weather along this remote Atlantic coast where the sea is never far away and often clearly visible. This stage to Muxía is slowly being discovered but still provides a sense of adventure. Around halfway we dip down into the beautiful Lires estuary that offers the only reasonably safe place for a swim and an opportunity for a midday break in the café/bar (if you plan to stay in the Xunta hostel in Muxía you need to collect a stamp *sello* here). A new footbridge over the Río do Castro has replaced the old stepping stones. Note – if the river is in high flood you may still need to take the detour by road via Pontenove (see map).

0.0 km From **Albergue ❸** in the centre of Finisterre, head up Calle Santa Catalina past the **Concello** and s/o at the junction of the **main road [0.4 km]** and turn up <left at **bus shelter [0.7 km]** (just beyond Hotel Arenal).

1.1 km **Arenal** *sign San Martiño de Duio* and first of the <Fisterra – Muxía> waymarks. Head up past Restaurante veering right> **[0.4 km]** where the road levels off to pass the delightful **San Martiño de Duio parish church [0.4 km]** and continue along the side of the Duio valley (site of the legendary city of Dugium) with fine sea views and turn up <left at **Escaselas crossroads [1.2 km]** through **Hermedesuxo [0.5 km]** down to the **crossroads [0.2 km]** and take the road signposted San Salvador and continue for **[0.4 km]** into:

3.1 km San Salvador *Hr*** Dugium €45-60 ✆ 981 740 780 offering rustic luxury in its restored interior. We now leave the road and head up onto a track through pine forest as it winds its way around alto Rapadoira. Continue s/o over the road at **Rial** down into **Buxán.**

2.6 km **Buxan** *Alb.* **Aurora** elevated site overlooking Buxan and the coast. Built

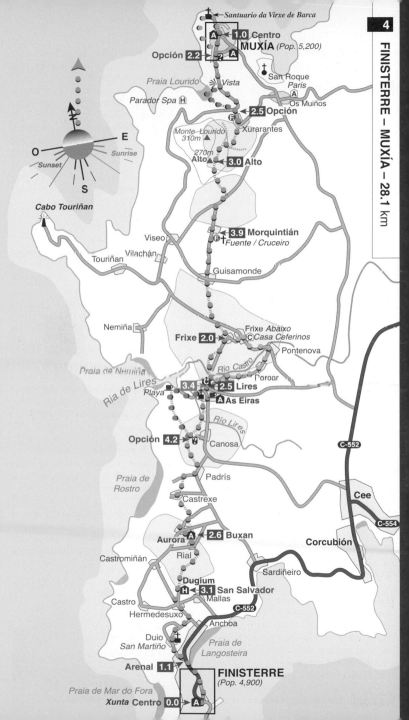

✝ ←*Santuario da Vírxe de Barca*

Ⓐ ◄ **1.0** Centro
MUXÍA *(Pop. 5,200)*

Opción ◄ **2.2**

Ⓐ

San Roque
Paris
✝

Praia Lourido ≈ *Vista*

Parador Spa Ⓗ

Os Muiños Ⓐ

◄ **2.5** Opción

Ⓕ

Monte Lourido Xurarantes
310m ▲

270m

▲ **Alto** ◄ **3.0** Alto

Ⓕ ✝ ◄ **3.9** Morquintián
Fuente / Cruceiro

Viseo

Cabo Touriñan ⚓

Vilachán
Guisamonde
Touriñan

Nemiña

Frixe *Abaixo*
Frixe ◄ **2.0** Ⓒ*Casa Ceferinos*

Pontenova

Praia de Nemiña

Río Castro

Ⓒ ◄ **2.5** Lires
3.4 Ⓒ Poroar

Playa Ⓐ **As Eiras**

Ria de Lires

Río Lires

Opción ◄ **4.2** ❓ Canosa

Praia de Rostro

Padrís

Castrexe

Cee

C-552

C-554

Aurora Ⓐ ◄ **2.6** Buxan

Corcubión

Castromiñán
Rial

Dugium
Ⓗ ◄ **3.1** San Salvador
Castro
Mallas
Sardiñeiro

Hermedesuxo
Anchoa
C-552

Duio ✝
San Martiño
Praia de Langosteira

Arenal **1.1** ▼

FINISTERRE
(Pop. 4,900)

Xunta Centro **0.0** → Ⓐ

Praia de Mar do Fora

O — E
Sunset *Sunrise*
S

in 2015 by cooperative in San Maritiño ✆ 981 750 707 (Marta) m: 609 041 590. Turn down <left and imm. right> out of the village and right> past timber yard and continue on asphalt road to next group of houses at **Suarriba** with the wild coast now clearly visible and turn <left [!] down wide track towards village below. **Castrexe** small hamlet and nearest point to Rostro beach. **Note**: *if you want to visit one of the remotest beaches in Galicia it is only 400 meters. Cool the feet but not the body – swimming along this coast is dangerous [!].* To continue to Muxía turn right> out of Castrexe and take the first track <left and right> at asphalt up into **Padrís** and veer <left onto delightful track through pine and eucalyptus woods to option point:

4.2 km **Opción*** The route is officially waymarked via **Canosa** but if the weather is reasonable and you have time (an extra ½ hour) the beautiful alternative option along the Lires estuary is recommended – adding just 1.3 km.

For alt. coastal route ● ● ● ● veer <left and proceed s/o along the walled lane (ignoring any turn-offs to left or right). The path enters the woodland ahead with fine views of the beautiful coastline to the west. The path winds down to join a well-maintained forestry track onto quiet asphalt road at the estuary of the river Lires with sandy beach that the locals use for swimming and Tapas Bar Playa (summer). *(If you intend to swim beware of changing tidal flows and river currents at any time of year – watch where the locals swim!).* Fishermen often line both banks of the estuary here which swirls with fish feeding off the local fish farm. The route now follows the road for another along the estuary to cross over the bridge to join up with the main route at the church of Saint Stephen at the entrance to Lires. Total distance of 3.4 km. (instead of 2.1 km).

For the main route continue s/o (right) at *option** point down to concrete lane through **Canosa** and turn left alongside the río Lires to join asphalt road into **Lires** at Iglesia San Esteban *Igrexa San estebo* with view of the *Ría de Lires* and the *Praia de Nemiña* where the alternative routes joins from the left. Turn right up into village:

2.5 km **Lires** *Centro* delightful village with café, pension new albergue + several casa rurales ± €40 as follows: *CR* **Raúl** ✆ 981 748 156 traditional building adj. church of San Esteban (*sello* in garden). *CR* **Lourido** ✆ 981 748 348 and towards the top end recently restored *CR* **Luz** ✆ 981 748 924 with welcome from Yolanda below the central crossroads and option.

Option ❖ the waymarked route veers left. *If you need refreshments or sello turn right for café/ bar / 100 metres and pension P* **As Eiras** +€30 ✆ 981 748 180 (Pablo) m: 662 261 818 and adj. new *Alb.* **As Eiras** *Priv.*[22÷4]+ €12 (photo right) with all facilities incl. bikes to explore the beach and barn with BBQ. Further up is *CR* **Jesús & Cabañas de Lires** ✆ 981 748 393. All facilities incl. swimming pool and gardens. Special price for pilgrims.

To continue turn <left at crossroads ❖ and veer right onto forest track down to a tributary of the **río Castro**. A new concrete bridge now satisfies the health and safety executive but eliminates the last 'funky' crossing via the original stepping stones still visible downstream. Cross river and head up track by **Bau Silbeiro** and continue s/o (an alternative route goes by the asphalt road right) veer right into woods to rejoin road and continue into Frixe.

2.0 km   Frixe *[right off route for casa rural CR* **Ceferinos** ℂ 981 748 965 *Lugar de Frixe Nº15 +½ km]*. Turn <left and imm. right> up onto path crossing over the **Touriñan road** *[The lighthouse at Cabo Touriñan is the most westerly point in Spain + 7.5 km west]*. Turn **down** <left and imm. right> by farm building and rejoin road at **Guisamonde** *(dogs)* into **Morquintián**.

3.9 km   Morquintián drinking font by *cruceiro*. Continue s/o and veer right up past houses and continue to **T-Junction** and turn right> [!] *(not the original waymarked route left)* and then take path <left up into woods. This next stretch is a delightful path that winds its way around the gorse-strewn slopes of **As Aferroas** and **Monte Facho de Lourido** with views over the Ría de Camariñas climbing gently towards today's high point *Alto (270m)*.

3.0 km   Alto the track now begins a gentle descent but zig zags down through the woodland so stay alert for waymarks into the village of **Xurarantes.** Turn <left and then right> down asphalt road passing fountain **Fuente** (left – with cool waters favoured by the locals) to T-junction and option point:

2.5 km   Road *Option:* The waymarked route turns right along the asphalt road all the way into Muxía *or...* continue s/o onto path for short detour over the sand dunes around **Playa de Lourido**. There are too many paths here to be specific but the shortest way is to take the right hand fork and make your way up along the boundary wall of a field (left) and large eucalyptus tree (right) onto sandy headland. At this point make your way

to the right over tidal mud flats to take the track back up to the main road visible above with panoramic view point **Punta de Vista** on the main road above Playa de Lourido. The new build on the headland is the latest Parador opening 2016. From here we follow the road along a bleak stretch of rocky coast past the town football ground to the Southern outskirts of Muxía.

2.2 km   Muxía *option* At the entrance to the town are several options: ❖ (see town plan):

[a] Continue s/o to the town centre, pilgrim office and central hostels [1.0 km] or
[b] Take the back road up right direct to the Xunta hostel [0.7 km] or
[c] Take the left (seaward) road direct to the *Sanctuario de Virxe da Barca* [1.5 km].

[a] ❖ S/o to **albergue [0.2** km] *Alb.* **❶ Da Costa** *Priv.*[8÷1]+ €10 +€30 ℂ 608 995 232 (Silvia y Carlos) Av. de Doctor Toba, 33. S/o to **park [0.2** km] and option point **[c]** ❖ *[to go to Sanctuario de Virxe da Barca veer left by coast into rúa Coido leading into rúa Atalaia (avoiding cul-de-sacs to the left) to the sanctuary [1.5 km].*

To continue to town centre **[a]** keep s/o into rua Areal veering right into **Rua Real [0.3** km] *P**** **Habitat /** *Hs* **Costa da Morte** ℂ 981 742 148 corner of Rúa Real and Eduardo Pondal and turn <left up the main street passing *H** **Casa Lorena** ℂ 981 742 564 who also run adj. wine bar *Vinoteca* on rúa Virxe da Barca,3 past the popular *P* **Pedra D'Abalar** ℂ 981 742 063 (adj. bar Prestige) into small plaza **[0.2** km] with *H*** **'a de loló'** €30-50 ℂ

981 742 422 boutique hotel and adj. ultra modern *Alb.*❷ **Bela Muxia [36÷2]**+ €12-15 priv. rooms +€40 ℂ 981 742 041 (Ángel Castro) m: 687 798 222 rúa Encarnación, 30 welcoming central hostel with all facilities + internet and extensive terraces overlooking the harbour. Note the entrance is *behind* the central tourist office 100 m further **[0.1** km**]**.

1.0 km Muxía *Centro Turismo* in the *Casa Cultura* rúa Virxe da Barca, 47 ℂ 981 742 563. The tourist office is also a pilgrim information centre and issues the **Muxíanna**, modelled on the *Fisterrana* and the *Compostela*, to pilgrims who have walked to Muxía from Santiago on presentation of a stamped credencial. In the event the office is closed albergue Bela Muxía to the rear is also licensed to issue the Muxianna and keeps detailed

information on bus schedules etc and has a bank of computers for internet searches.

[b] ❖ Take the 'back' road direct to the Xunta hostel **[0.7** km]. Turn up right> at the option (imm. past house no: 45 point at the entrance to Muxía) to T-junction and turn up right> into **rúa Os Malatos [0.2** km] past Guardia Civil to top of road which curves to the left and continue to T-junction **[0.5** km] and *Alb.*❸ **Xunta [32÷2]** €6 ultra-modern concrete building at the top of rúa Enfesto at the southern side of town with good modern facilities in utilitarian style building with large reception area.

Other Lodging: *Alb.*❹ **@Muxía** *Priv.*[40÷2] €11 ℂ 981 742 118 (José) m: 651 627 768 c/Enfesto, 12 just below the Xunta hostel. Closeby on the seafront *Alb.*❺ **Delphin [15÷2]** €6 ℂ 622 345 358 quiet ambience with Hungarian associations on rúa Marina. Closeby along the seafront *P**** **La Cruz** ℂ 981 742 084 Av. López Abente,44. *P* **Casa Isolina** ℂ 981 742 367 m: 630581 744 on c/Real,52 (family operate Bar Wimpe on the harbour front). **Arrivada** ℂ 981 742 112 c/José María del Río,30. *Outside* town (0.7 km from La Cruz): *P** **O Rincón da Baiuca** ℂ 981 742 583 Largo da Baiuca. A number of private houses may also offer accommodation (not on any official list – look for signs on windows). Choice of restaurants and bars around the harbour area and town centre. *O Porto* and *A Pedra d'Abalar* meson: ℂ 981 742 063 (also operates the pension).

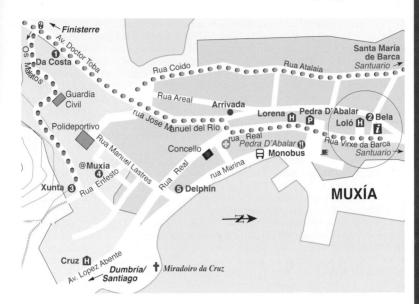

Return to Santiago: *Monbus* © 902 292 900 & Ferrín 981 870 965 check schedule at tourist office or bus-stop on rúa Marina (generally from 06:45 – 14:30 later on Sunday). *Taxi* © 981 742 070 Santiago (± 1 hour) €60.

Muxía: Fishing port with a (declining) population of 5,200 that, along with Finisterre, seems to have made the most of the poor economic climate that has blighted much of rural Galicia. Despite the harsh Atlantic weather that beats against its shores it looks brighter now than it did some years ago. Houses have been renovated, the college upgraded and 4 new pilgrim hostels completed. Apart from summer tourism the mainstay of the town has been the modern fishing fleet that hums with activity from the rich fishing grounds offshore. A walk around the harbour and through the old town will acquaint you with an authentic Galician fishing village. It is easy to get lost in the narrow streets that run between rúa Atalaia on the west and rúas Real and Virxe da Barca to the east – use the sun to orientate yourself or enjoy the 'lostness'. The name Muxía is derived from *Mongía* land of monks from the nearby 12thC Romanesque monastic church San Xulián de Moraime. These monks came here in 1105 in an effort to suppress the pagan rituals that were being practised at that time.

Muxía's main claim to fame and the reason why it is so intimately connected to the Santiago story is to be found in the legend of **Our Lady of the Boat** *Nosa Señora da Barca* and the Sanctuary at the headland *Santuario da Virxe da Barca* located at the far end of town (due North). A popular pilgrimage site in its own right and associated with the Virgin Mary who, the legend claims, came here in a boat made of stone to help St. James in his ministry. St. James, feeling that he had failed in his mission to convert the population of Finisterre from their worship of the sun, travelled to this remote place for rest and succour. As he prayed he saw a boat with the Virgin Mary aboard, 'full of mystery and majesty', approaching the headland. The Virgin assured him that his ministry had in fact been successful and that his work here was done and he should return to Jerusalem.

Legend tells us that the boat in which she travelled became petrified in the stones we see here on the headland. The most obvious is the stone sail *Pedra dos Cadris* (see photo below) which reputedly has miraculous powers of healing – pass under the stone 9 times to be cured of rheumatism and associated ailments. The rudder stone *Pedra do Timón* and rocking hull *Pedra da Abalar* are nearby. This latter stone moves on its axis and was used to prove innocence or guilt of any accused brought before it. It was cracked during a storm in 1978 but its powers of attraction remain undiminished. Nearby is the lovers' stone *Pedra dos Namorados* where couples come to pledge their love.

Watching over all this activity is the austere 17th century sanctuary dedicated to the Virgin. Originally founded in the 12th century on a pre-Christian site It was hit by a lightening strike on Christmas day 2013 and severely damaged by the ensuing fire but has been rebuilt. You can approach it either via option **[c]** (previous page) known as the Way of the Skin *Camiño da Pel.* So called because a fountain here was used by pilgrims to wash and purify themselves before entering the sanctuary or via rúa Marina along the harbour front. Both routes are 1.5 km (0.7 km from the tourist office). Just above the sanctuary by the stone monument is another smaller paved path that goes to the top of the conical hillock *Monte Corpiño* 81 metres high and a 400m climb to the top where there is a fine 360° view of the town, the harbour, coastline with *Camariñas* (famous for its fine handmade lace) across the bay and the hamlet of *Chorente* on the wooded headland through which the path to Dumbria passes (stage 5 / 5a). To return to the town centre take the rúa Virxe da Barca that connects the sanctuary with the harbour area. Along this way is the 14th century parish church of Saint Mary *Iglesia de Santa Maria* built in the coastal-Gothic style *gótica-marinero.* A major pilgrimage *Romaría da Virxe da Barca* takes place every year in September.

Note: Maps in these guides are one-directional so the reverse maps are included for those returning by foot to Santiago via Finisterre in an anti-clockwise direction (see pages 118-121):

REFLECTIONS:

_____
_____
_____
_____
_____
_____
_____
_____
_____
_____
_____
_____
_____
_____
_____
_____
_____
_____
_____
_____
_____
_____
_____
_____
_____
_____

Muxia harbour front from miradoiro de cruz

❏ **Life must be lived forwards, but can only be understood backwards.**

Kierkegaard

5   MUXÍA – OLVEIROA *via DUMBRIA*

▦▦▦▦▦	--- ---	15.9 --- ---	49%
▬▬▬	--- ---	16.4 --- ---	51%
▬▬▬	--- ---	0.0 --- ---	0%
Total km		**32.3** km *(20.1 ml)*	

36.5 km (^850m = 4.2 km)
Alto ▲   Hospital 385 m   (1,263 ft)
< 🄰 🄷 >   Os Muinos **5.2** km – Ozón **9.4** km
Quintáns **10.8** – Dumbría **21.8** km – Hospital **27.4** km – Logoso **28.8** km

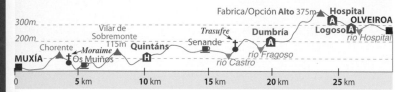

❏ **The Practical Path:** Another long stage but half is on forest tracks through woodland that provides shelter and new interim hostels provide options to break the journey. The route has been changed over the years so extra vigilance is required. Use the sun-compass to help with orientation and avoid arrows in the *opposite* direction. Take water and snack food.

0.0 km   **Centro** from the town centre (*Alb.*❷ **Bela Muxía**) head south along Rúa Mariña past Miradoiro da Cruz and turn <left onto a board-walk that skirts the edge of the *praia Espiñeirido* cross s/o over road at far end onto **woodland path [1.6 km]** and up steeply through woods around *Monte de Chorente* with views back over Muxía and the wide bay *Ría Camariñas* and *Cabo Vilán.* Continue along walled lane to the village of **Chorente [1.0** km] veer right> and right> again then up <left to our high point of this section at the chapel of Saint Roch **[0.6** km].

3.2 km   **Capela de San Roque** – pleasant woodland rest area with cruceiro. Head downhill over main road and onto the old road and turn right> and then immediately <left downhill and take the next <left past the ancient *fonte* to the 12[th]century Romanesque church of St. Julian *Igrexa de St. Xulián de Moraime* in **Moraime [0.8** km]. The original monastery established by Benedictine monks gave rise to the name 'land of monks' *Mongía* or *Muxía.* The monastery no longer exists but the ancient church keeps the connection. Continue diagonally over the park and take the steps down over the main road again by ruined house onto rough path veering right> down to secondary road and up into Os Muiños **[1.2** km].

2.0 km   **Os Muiños** *The Mills* small town with good facilities. The waymarked route brings us behind the village to avoid the main road by turning up <left by *farmacia* and then down by *panadería* over the **río Negro** passing turnoff (left) to local river walk *paseo fluvial* and turnoff (right) to cafe/pension *P'* **Paris** ℂ 981 740 616. Continue to end of village and turn <left in the direction of Merexo *(camping 5km sign)* **[0.4** km]. This quiet road meanders through pine forest to veer off **right> [1.4** km] *[Note: Merexo s/o + 0.6 km with Hs Praia de Lago ℂ 981 750 793 + 2 km].*

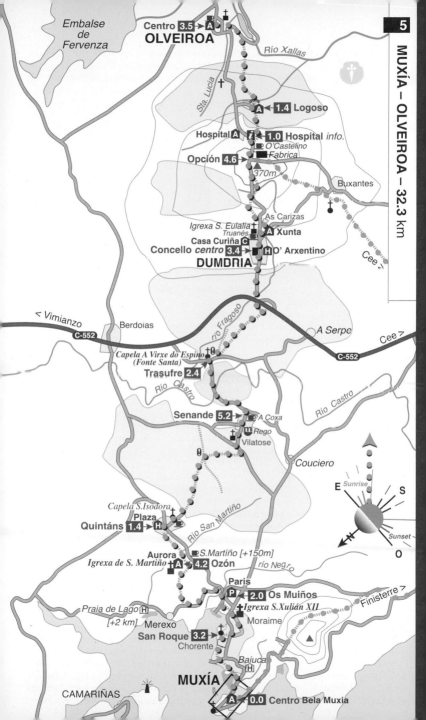

Embalse de Fervenza

Centro 3.5 → A
OLVEIROA

Río Xallas

Sta. Lucía

A ← 1.4 **Logoso**

Hospital A ← 1.0 **Hospital** *info.*
O'Castelino
Fabrica
Opción 4.6 →
▲ *370m*

Buxantes

As Carizas

Igrexa S. Eulalia
Truanés A **Xunta**
Casa Curiña C
Concello *centro* 3.4 → H **O' Arxentino**
DUMBRIA

Cee

< Vimianzo **Berdoias**
río Fragoso
A Serpe
C-552
Cee >

Capela A Virxe do Espino
(Fonte Santa)
Trasufre 2.4

Río Castro

Río Castro

Senande 5.2 → *A Coxa*
Rego
Vilatose
Couciero

Rio San Martiño

Capela S.Isodora
Plaza
Quintáns 1.4 → H

Aurora
Igrexa de S. Martiño A 4.2 **Ozón**
S.Martiño [+150m]
río Negro

Paris
P 2.0 **Os Muiños**
Igrexa S.Xulián XII
Finisterre >

Praia de Lago H
[+2 km] **Merexo**
San Roque 3.2
Moraime
Chorente

Baiuca
H

MUXÍA

CAMARIÑAS

A 0.0 **Centro Bela Muxia**

E Sunrise S
Sunset
O

The path turns up right> around side of house onto a wide forest track that winds its way up through dense pine woods around *Pena da Serra* alto (150m) continue s/o at cross of 5 tracks and turn <left on road in the aptly named **Vilar de Sobremonte** [**1.5** km]. The route now zig-zags sharp right> to the parish church of San Martiña de Ozón and the adj. monastery now coming back to life as an albergue [**0.9** km]

4.2 km **Monasterio de San Martiño de Ozón** *Alb.* **Aurora de los Caminos** *Priv.*[12÷2] €-donation *©* 981 750 707 (Marta) m: 609 041 590. Former 12th century monastery currently undergoing renovations through a cooperative venture with the basic aim to live more lightly on the planet with respect for planet and people. The community is largely made up of pilgrims who simply 'arrived and never left'. Turn down <left by wayside

cross onto an ancient cobbled street with one of Galicia's longest granaries *horreos* with 22 pairs of granite supports which is also part of the albergue and now 'stores' volunteers working in the community. Short 150m detour (right) to *café* San Martiño on the main road. *Stay focused [!] on this next stretch that twists its way into Quintáns on quiet country lanes and farm tracks.* Continue over the **río San Martiño** and s/o track over road turning <left and imm. right> onto another track by wayside cross. S/o over road veering right past farm buildings into:

1.4 km **Quintáns Plaza Maior** town with good facilities on the AC-440 with several café/bars and lodging at the *P*° **Plaza** *©* 981 750 452 in the main square presided over by Isaac. From here the path continues over the main road up past *café* D'arriba (right) and Capella de San Isodora (left) s/o at crossroads and imm. <left onto wide track and s/o (ignoring paths to left or right) to top of rise and keeps s/o through eucalyptus woods and turn <left on **road** [**4.1** km] and next right> into **Vilastose** [**0.4** km] Igrexa San Cibrán (with separate bell tower) and turn <left at crossroads up into Senande [**0.7** km].

5.2 km **Senande** *Bar-Tienda* Casa Rego turn right> at crossroads down the main street past *Bar* A Picola and pilgrim-friendly *café* A Coxa where Jesús will serve you a drink while his mother Pilar might be coaxed into preparing one of the best omelettes in Galicia! *Stay focused [!] on this next section which criss-crosses several roads.* Just past the bar veer s/o <left onto minor road (pista polideportiva) and turn **<left [0.9** km] to T-junction imm. ahead and turn right> and continue along quiet road turning <left at next T-junction down over *Rio Castro* [**1.1** km] (whose waters we crossed in Lires) and up to the roadside chapel [**0.4** km].

2.4 km **Trasufre** chapel of Our Lady of Espiño *Capela A Virxe do Espiño* (also known as Santuario de N.S de Aránzazu) and below it the Holy Fountain *Fonte Santa* whose waters are said to have healing powers. *[You will find pieces of cloth tied to the hedgerow here – a local tradition going back centuries whereby pilgrims come to this shrine for healing by leaving behind unwanted ailments to disintegrate along with the cloth that is their symbolic representation – do not tidy up!].*

Follow the road up right past cruceiro and water tap (left) to turn off **<left [0.3** km] [!] onto track and imm. right> by modern horreo onto narrow path around the right hand (southerly) side of the hill. The path is steep but has been well surfaced and meanders through delightful woodland up to the main road [**1.3** km]. Here turn down <left on a path parallel to the main AC-552 to cross over [!] onto the old road over **Río Fragoso** up s/o at roundabout [**1.0** km] past bus-stop (left) turn right at next roundabout into the centre of Dumbría [**0.8** km].

3.4 km   **Dumbría** *Casa Consistorial Concello Pensión* O Arxentino ℂ 981 744 051 €35 on side road opp. the Concello with restaurant, bar and shop. Continue past the concello on main road *[turn (left) to CR* **Curiña** *€48-60 (check opening dates)* ℂ *981 744 024 m: 659 734 321 on c/ Estiman].* *Bar-supermecado* Truanés ℂ 981 744 079. **Dumbria:** declining population currently 3,300. There is an

interesting chronological display outside the concello which records the history of the area. Daily bus connection to Santiago Vasquez coaches at 8:40 and 14:25 with change in Bayo – check schedule updates at Bar Truanés. Taxi service Jesús ℂ 981 748 188 m: 647 236 701.

Continue along main road past **Iglesia de Santa Eulalia** (left) and down to the bottom of the hill and turn right> past play area and to the rear of the sports centre **polideportivo [0.6** km] and *Alb.* **Xunta [26÷4]** €6 ℂ 981 744 001 (Concello de Dumbria) ultra modern pilgrim hostel with all facilities built with funds from Galician economic hero Amancio Ortega. The path now takes a right turn into woodland and s/o at crossroads up into the hamlet of **As Carizas [1.0** km] and imm. up sharp <left onto concrete path that shortly continues as steep pathway through woodland and turn right> on **main road [0.2** km] (*not* path s/o). Beware of traffic on the dangerous bend [!]) and turn up < left [0,4 km] onto woodland path to cross back over main road again and over the headwaters of the *rio Fragoso*, now little more than a trickle, and back up to **main road [1.1** km]. Now it's all the way back to the factory at Hospital visible on the horizon and option point [**1.3** km].

4.6 km   Option / Crossroads. *Note: This is the original option point to Finisterre or Muxía.* If you have walked from Santiago as part of the camino Finisterre / Muxía circuit the route will now appear familiar as we return to Santiago from this point *in reverse*: Pass *Café / Alb.* O' Castelino [**0.6** km] down to Hospital [**0.4**km].

1.0 km   **Hospital** Pilgrim information centre. *Alb.* ❶ Hospital *Priv.[22÷3]* €12 ℂ 981 747 387 (300m *off* route) *down* main road and cross over into the village where the hostel is on located at the lower end. To continue turn right> and imm. <left at info. centre down into Logoso:

1.4 km   **Logoso** *Café / Alb.* **Logoso** *Priv.[20÷3]*+ €12 €30 in pension ℂ 981 727 602 (Domingo) m: 659 505 399. Continue down over *Rio do Hospital* and along the forest track back down over *Rego do Santa Lucia* and up past the casa rural *Pr***·** **As Pías** €40-60 ℂ 981 741 520 m: 617 026 005to the central hostels in Olveiroa.

3.5 km   **Olveiroa** *Alb.* ❶ Hórreo *Priv.[53÷5]*+ €12 ℂ 981 741 673 adj. *CR* **Casa Loncho** rooms from €40. *Alb.* ❷ Olveiroa *Xunta.[46÷5]* €6 ℂ 658 045 242.

We continue back to Santiago via Negreira following routes 2 and 1 *in reverse*. *Note:* maps in these guides are one-directional so the reverse maps are included on the following pages 116 & 117. Pilgrims walking the route in an *anti-clockwise* direction from Hospital – Muxía – Finisterre – Hospital see maps on pages 119–121.

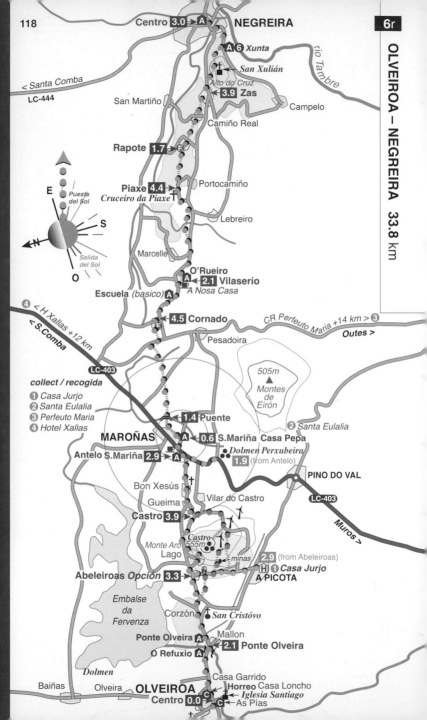

Centro **3.0** → A   **NEGREIRA**

A 6 *Xunta*

† *San Xulián*
Alto do Cruz
← **3.9** Zas

< Santa Comba
LC-444

San Martiño

Campelo

Camiño Real

Rapote 1.7 → R

Portocamiño

E
Puesta del Sol

Piaxe 4.4 →
Cruceiro da Piaxe

Lebreiro

S

Marcelle

O'Rueiro

Salida del Sol

O

A **2.1** Vilaserío
R
A Nosa Casa

Escuela (basico) A

← **4.5** Cornado
R

Pesadoira

CR Perfeuto Maria +14 km > ❸

Outes >

❹ < H.Xallas +12 km

< S.Comba

505m
▲
Montes de Eirón

LC-403

collect / recogida
❶ Casa Jurjo
❷ Santa Eulalia
❸ Perfeuto Maria
❹ Hotel Xallas

← **1.4** **Puente**

A ← **0.6** S.Mariña **Casa Pepa**

❷ Santa Eulalia

MAROÑAS

Dolmen Perxubeira
1.9 (from Antelo)

Antelo S.Mariña 2.9 → A

PINO DO VAL

Bon Xesús †

Vilar do Castro

Gueima

LC-403

Castro 3.9 →

Muros >

Monte Aro
Castro 555m

Lago

minas **2.9** (from Abeleiroas)

Ⓗ ❶ *Casa Jurjo*

Abeleiroas *Opción* **3.3** →

A **PICOTA**

Embalse da Fervenza

Corzón ‖ *San Cristóvo*

Mallon

Ponte Olveira A
2.1 Ponte Olveira

O Refuxio A

Dolmen

Baiñas   Olveira

Casa Garrido
Horreo Casa Loncho
Iglesia Santiago

OLVEIROA
Centro **0.0** → C
C ← As Pías

†

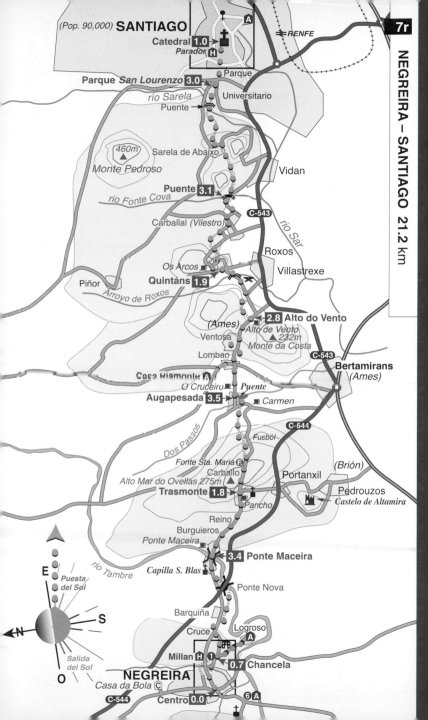

(Pop. 90,000) **SANTIAGO**

Catedral 1.0 →

Parador H

≈ RENFE

Parque *San Lourenzo* **3.0**

Parque

río Sarela

Universitario

Puente →

460m

Sarela de Abaixo

Monte Pedroso

Vidan

río Fonte Cova

Puente 3.1

C-543

Carballal (Vilestro)

río Sar

Roxos

Villastrexe

Os Arcos

Quintáns 1.9

Piñor

Arroyo de Roxos

2.8 Alto do Vento

(Ames)

Alto de Vento

Ventosa ▲ 232m

Monte da Costa

Lombao

C-543

Bertamirans

(Ames)

Casa Riamonte A

O Cruceiro **Puente**

Augapesada 3.5 →

Carmen

C-544

Dos Passos

Fusbol

Fonte Sta. Maria

Alto Mar do Ovellas 275m

Carballo

(Brión)

Portanxil

Trasmonte 1.8

Pancho

Pedrouzos

Castelo de Altamira

Reino

Burguieros

Ponte Maceira

3.4 Ponte Maceira

Capilla S. Blas

Ponte Nova

Barquiña

Cruce

Logroso

A

Millan H 1

0.7 Chancela

NEGREIRA

Casa da Bola C

C-544

Centro 0.0

6 A

E

Puesta del Sol

S

N

Salida del Sol

O

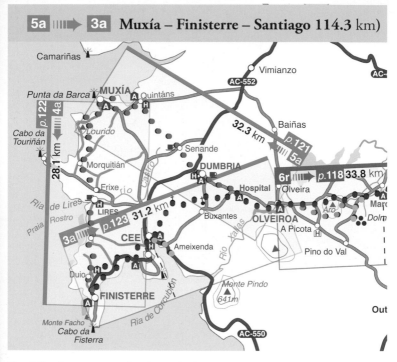

5a ⫸ 3a **Muxía – Finisterre – Santiago 114.3** km)

Camariñas

Vimianzo

AC-552

Punta da Barca **MUXÍA** Quintáns

Lourido

Baiñas **32.3 km** *p.121* 5a

Cabo da Touriñán **28.1 km** 4a

Senande

DUMBRÍA

Morquitián **6r** ⫸ *p.118* **33.8 km**

Frixe **Hospital** Olveira

Río Castro

LIRES *p.123* **31.2 km** **OLVEIROA** Aro *Dolm*

Praia Rostro Buxantes A Picota

CEE Ameixenda Río Xalas Pino do Val

Duio

Monte Pindo 641m

FINISTERRE

Monte Facho **Cabo da Fisterra** Ria de Corcubión

AC-550

Out

The following maps are for those pilgrims walking the circuit in the alternative ***anti-clockwise*** direction; from Olveiroa (Hospital) to Muxía *[map 5a]* – Muxía to Finisterre *[map 4a]* – Finisterre to Olveiroa *[map 3a]*. Details of accommodation are listed in the appropriate pages as in the clockwise journey.

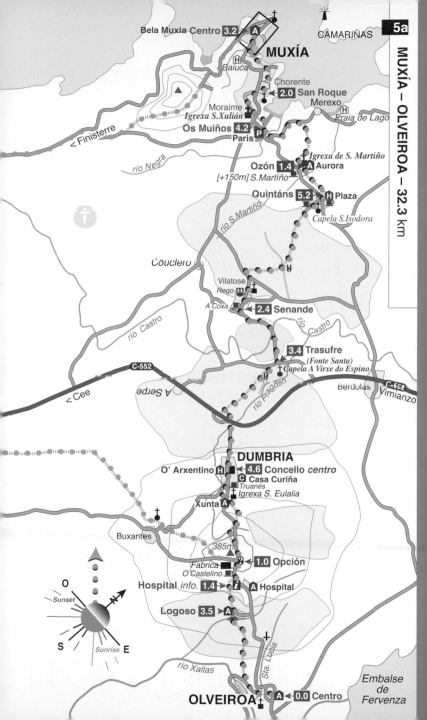

MUXÍA

CAMARIÑAS

Bela Muxia Centro **3.2** → **A**

Baiuca ⊞

Chorente
2.0 ← San Roque
Merexo
Praia de Lago ⊞

Moraime
Igrexa S.Xulián
Os Muiños **4.2**
Paris **P**

< Finisterre

río Negra

Igrexa de S. Martiño
Ozón **1.4** **A** Aurora
[+150m] *S.Martiño*

Quintáns **5.2** → ⊞ Plaza

Capela S.Isodora

río S.Martiño

Couclero

Vilatose
Rego m
A Coxa **2.4** Senande

río Castro

río Castro

3.4 Trasufre
(Fonte Santa)
Capela A Virxe do Espino

C-552
< Cee   *A Serpe* *río Fragden*   Berdolas
Vimianzo   C-552

DUMBRIA

O' Arxentino ⊞ **4.6** Concello *centro*
C Casa Curiña
Truanés
Igrexa S. Eulalia
Xunta **A**

Buxantes

385m
▲
Fabrica
O'Castelino   **1.0** Opción

Hospital *info.* **1.4** **i** **A** Hospital

Logoso **3.5** → **A**

O
Sunset
S   E
Sunrise

río Xallas
Sta. Lucia

OLVEIROA   **A** ← **0.0** Centro

Embalse
de
Fervenza

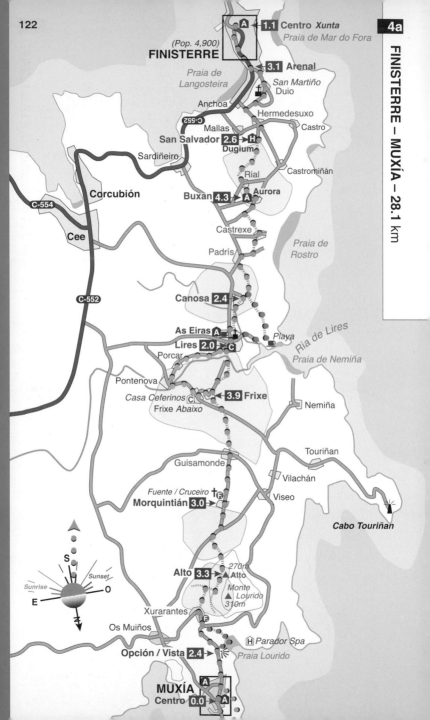

A **1.1** Centro *Xunta*
Praia de Mar do Fora

(Pop. 4,900)
FINISTERRE

3.1 Arenal

Praia de Langosteira

San Martiño Duio

Anchoa

Hermedesuxo

Mallas

Castro

San Salvador 2.6 **H**
Dugium

Sardiñeiro

Castromiñán

Rial

Corcubión

Buxán **4.3** **A** Aurora

Cee

Castrexe

Padrís

Praia de Rostro

Canosa **2.4**

As Eiras **A**

Lires **2.0** **C**

Playa

Ría de Lires

Porcar

Praia de Nemiña

Pontenova

Casa Ceferinos **C** **3.9** Frixe

Frixe *Abaixo*

Nemiña

Touriñan

Guisamonde

Vilachán

Fuente / Cruceiro †**F**
Morquintián **3.0** **F**

Viseo

Cabo Touriñan

S

Sunset

Sunrise

270m
Alto **3.3** ▲ Alto

Monte Lourido 310m

E

O

Xurarantes **F**

Os Muiños

H *Parador Spa*

Opción / Vista **2.4**

Praia Lourido

MUXÍA
Centro **0.0** **A**

A

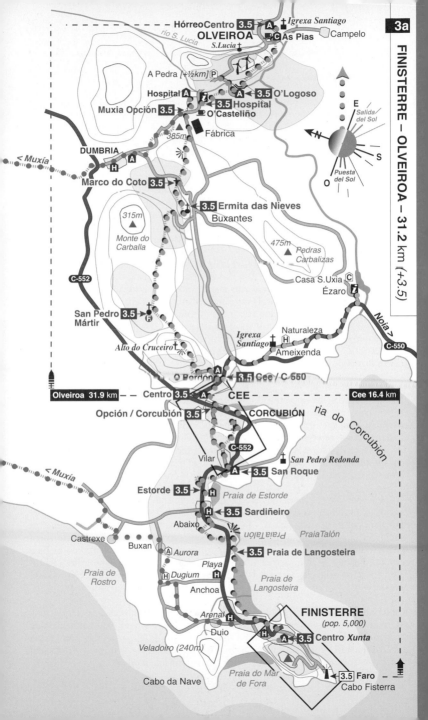

HórreoCentro **3.5** ← **A** ← † *Igrexa Santiago*
OLVEIROA **C** As Pias ☐ Campelo
S.Lucia †

A Pedra *[+½km]* **P**

Hospital **A** **i** **A** ← **3.5** O'Logoso
Muxia Opción **3.5** → **3.5** Hospital
O'Casteliño
▲ *385m* ☐ Fábrica

DUMBRIA
H **A**
< Muxía

Marco do Coto **3.5** †

3.5 Ermita das Nieves
315m Buxantes
▲
Monte do
Carballa *475m*
▲ *Pedras*
Carbalizas

C-552

Casa S.Uxia **C**
Éxaro **i**

San Pedro **3.5** †
Mártir **F**

Alto do Cruceiro †

Igrexa Naturaleza
Santiago ■ **H**
Ameixenda

Noia >

C-550

Olveiroa **31.9 km** – – Centro **3.5** ← **A** **CEE** – – – – – Cee **16.4 km**
O Bordón → **3.5** Cee / C 550

Opción / Corcubión **3.5** **CORCUBIÓN** *ria do Corcubión*

C-552

Vilar ■ *San Pedro Redonda*
A ← **3.5** San Roque

Estorde **3.5** **H** *Praia de Estorde*
H ← **3.5** Sardiñeiro
Abaixo *Praia Talón* *PraiaTalón*
Castrexe
Buxan **A** *Aurora*
Playa **3.5** Praia de Langosteira
H *Dugium* **H**
Praia de Anchoa *Praia de*
Rostro *Langosteira*

Arenal **H**
Duio **H** **A** ← **3.5**
Veladoiro (240m) **FINISTERRE**
(pop. 5,000)
Centro *Xunta*
Cabo da Nave *Praia do Mar* ▲
de Fora **3.5** Faro
Cabo Fisterra

rio S. Lucia
E
Salida
del Sol
N
O S
Puesta
del Sol

❐ *The breeze at dawn has something to tell you. Don't go back to sleep.* Rumi

RETURNING HOME: *Some inner thoughts ...*

It is likely that your outer appearance might have changed but it is also possible that the way you perceive the world has gone through some metamorphosis. This inner transformation may well deepen as the lessons we learnt along the way become more fully integrated. While an obvious purpose of pilgrimage is to bring about an inner shift, it is also possible that our familiar world will no longer support this inner change. This realisation might engender different emotions as we come to see that choices may have to be made that could alter our previous way of life – what we do, where we work, who we live with, our social circuit, where and how we pray or meditate. Indeed the whole purpose, focus and direction of our life may have altered. This may be intimidating to those who previously knew us *the way we were.* Change threatens the status quo but the biggest challenge may be to hold fast to our new understanding garnered from the insights we learnt along the way.

Whatever our individual experiences it is likely that we will be in a heightened state of consciousness and sensitivity. We should resist squeezing our itinerary and the feeling we need to rush back into our usual pattern of work and general lifestyle – this can be a crucial moment. How often do we witness change in ourselves and others only to see fear come and rob us of our new understanding and orientation. Perhaps this is the time to revisit the Self-assessment questionnaire and recall the original purpose and intention of our pilgrimage. If this was (for example) to 'come closer to God', then we should not be surprised if everything that could get in the way of that high invocation is removed from our life, or at least challenged!

Essentially, we are all on a journey of rediscovery of our Essential Nature – our spiritual reality as we begin opening to the knowledge of Higher Worlds. Remember that we have collectively been asleep a long time. While change *can* happen in the twinkling of an eye, it is often experienced as a slow and painful process. The main challenge to our new perspective is likely to be the twin demons of fear and lethargy. The extent to which we hold onto a new way of looking at the world is measured by how far we are prepared to hold onto our truth in the face of opposition – often from those who profess to love us – by such was Christ crucified.

Of course our inner changes may not be so dramatic or those around us may likewise be engaged in inner work and so, far from feeling threatened, may welcome your shift with open arms and hearts – in this case you are blessed indeed. However, it would still be well to remember that these supportive others may not have spent weeks walking an ancient spiritual path surrounded by the silence of nature. Take time to integrate back into your life and nurture yourself. Build up a network of fellow pilgrims who can empathise with how you might be feeling and can actively support you.

Know that change is nearly always seen as threat within consensus society. Know also that if you try and change another to your new viewpoint you can aggravate the sense of loss and alienation felt by that other – this is all part of the journey and grist for the mill. Ultimately you can only be responsible for your own actions and re-actions. You cannot be responsible for the experience of others.

This guidebook is dedicated to awakening beyond human consciousness. It was born out of an existential crisis and the perceived need for a time to reflect on the purpose of life and its direction. Collectively devoid of inner-connectedness and a sense of the sacred, we live in a spiritual vacuum of our own making. While ensnared by our outer-directed materialistic world, we unwittingly hold the key to the door of our self-made prison. We can walk free any time we choose. We have been so long separated from our divine origins that we have forgotten what freedom feels like. In our fear of the unknown we choose to limit the potential of each new day to the familiarity of our prison surroundings. Perhaps *El Camino* will reveal the key to your own inner awakening.

As you take a well deserved rest at the end of the long road to the end of the way the question might well arise, 'Is the journey over or just beginning?' Whatever answer you receive will doubtless be right for you at this time. I wish you well in your search for the Truth and your journey Home and extend my humble blessings to a fellow pilgrim on the path and leave you with the words of *J R R Tolkein* from The Lord of the Rings:

> *The Road goes ever on and on*
> *Down from the door where it began.*
> *Now far ahead the Road has gone,*
> *And I must follow, if I can,*
> *Pursuing it with wary feet,*
> *Until it joins some larger way,*
> *Where many paths and errands meet.*
> *And whither then? I cannot say.*

A tithe of all royalties from the sale of this book will be distributed to individuals or organisations seeking to preserve the physical and spiritual integrity of this route.

Much of the information given here comes from local information garnered along the way. Myth and legend abound and, while frequently arising from some historical occurrence they are, by their very nature, not dependent on fact. If you are interested to find additional sources that referred to the importance of Finisterre as a place of spiritual transformation – try your local library or search the internet.

Bibliography:

The Bible in Spain, by George Borrow. Originally published London, 1842

A Stranger in Spain, by H.V Morton. Methuen: London, 1955.

Nine Faces of Christ, by Eugene Whitworth. DeVorss 1993.

A Course In Miracles, Foundation for Inner Peace. Penguin Books 1975

Poems – Rosalía de Castro, translated by Anna-Marie Aldaz, Barbara N. Gantt and Anne C. Bromley. State University of New York Press, 1991.

As Pegadas de Santiago na Cultura de Fisterra, by Benjamin Trillo Trillo. Fundación Caixa Galicia, 1999. (Trilingual: Galego, Castellano, English)

O Camiño de Fisterra, by Fernando Alonso Romero. Edicións Xerais de Galicia, 1993 (Trilingual: Galego, Castellano, English)

Mar Tenebroso – A costa da morte do sol, Ramón Allegue Martínez. EuroGraficas pichel,1996. (Galego)

Galicia Enteira – Fisterra e Costa da Morte, Xosé Luís Laredo Verdejo. Edicións Xerais de Galicia, 1996. (Galego)

El Camino del Milenio, Ramón Allegue Martínez. Baupres Editores, 2000.

O Camiño dos Peregrinos á Fin do Mundo, Antón Pombo y otros. Deputación Provincial da Coruña, 2000. (Galego)

The Fisterra-Muxía Way, Manuel Rodríguez. Xunta de Galicia, pamphlet 2007.

Useful Addresses:

UK: The Confraternity of St. James – **www.csj.org.uk**

IRELAND: The Irish Society of the Friends of St. James – **www.stjamesirl.com**

U.S.A. American Pilgrims on the Camino – **www.americanpilgrims.com**

CANADA: Canadian Company of Pilgrims Canada – **www.santiago.ca**

SOUTH AFRICA: Confraternity of St. James of SA – **www.csjofsa.za.org**

GALICIA: The Galician association AGACS – **www.amigosdelcamino.com**

Latest news (formerly Santiago-Today) – **www.caminodesantiago.me**

Stamps *Sellos* are readily available from hostels, churches, council and tourist offices, bars and cafés. Apart from authenticating your pilgrim status they make an interesting record of your travels. Ideally you will be a member of your local confraternity and already have an official *credencial* which can be obtained in either Sarria or Santiago. You need 2 stamps a day to apply for a Compostela in Santiago.

12 Caminos de Santiago

❶ Camino Francés 790 km
St. Jean / Roncesvalles – Santiago

❷ Chemin de Paris 1000 km
Paris – St. Jean via Orléans &Tours
Alt. route from Chartres -
Soulac – Tarnos 170km

❸ Chemin de Vézelay 900 km
Vezélay – St. Jean via Bazas
Ext. to Namur (B) & Maastricht (NL)

❹ Chemin de Le Puy 740 km
Le Puy-en-Velay – St. Jean
Ext. to Geneva, Konstanz, Prague

❺ Chemin d'Arles 750 km
Arles – Somport Pass
Camino Aragonés 160 km
Somport Pass – Óbanos
Camí San Jaume 600 km
Port de Selva – Jaca

❻ Camino de Madrid 320km
Madrid – Sahagún

Camino de Levante 900 km
Valencia (Alicante) – Zamora
Alt. via Cuenca – Burgos

❼ Camino Mozárabe 390km
Granada – Mérida
(Málaga alt. via Baena)

❽ Via de la Plata 1,000km
Seville – Santiago

❾ Camino Portugués *Central* 241km
Lisboa – Porto
Porto – Santiago

Camino Portugués *da Costa* 372km
Porto – Caminho
A Guarda – Redonela

❿ Camino Finisterre 87km
Santiago – Finisterre
via – Muxía – Santiago 114 km

⓫ Camino Inglés 110km
Ferrol – Santiago

⓬ Camino del Norte 830km
Irún – Santiago via Gijón
Camino Primitivo 320km
Oviedo – Lugo – Melide